drum circle:
A Guide to World Percussion

Chalo Eduardo & Frank Kumor

Includes:

- Cultural History & Significance
- Performance Techniques
- Enhanced CD with Audio/Visual Tutorials
- New & Traditional Ensemble Arrangements
- Traditional Notation & Contemporary Time Unit Box Notation

Alfred Music Publishing Co., Inc.
P.O. Box 10003
Van Nuys, CA 91410-0003
alfred.com

ISBN-10: 0-7390-2308-X (Book)
ISBN-13: 978-0-7390-2308-2 (Book)

ISBN-10: 0-7390-2309-8 (Book & CD)
ISBN-13: 978-0-7390-2309-9 (Book & CD)

ISBN-10: 0-7390-2319-5 (CD)
ISBN-13: 978-0-7390-2319-8 (CD)

Cover photos courtesy of Remo, Inc.

contents

About the Enhanced CD

The Drum Circle enhanced CD (#20611) doubles as a fun multimedia learning tool that works on any Windows-compatible or Macintosh computer. The CD includes all the written musical exercises and rhythms, as well as great audio/visual demonstrations that can be slowed down for practice purposes.

foreword

The exponential growth of hand drumming as well as world percussion over the past few years has created a widespread availability of instruments, yet a minimum of instructional materials. The challenge in this genre is that of producing educational materials that can serve on a variety of levels. Chalo Eduardo and Frank Kumor have succeeded in presenting a comprehensive approach to world percussion instruments and authentic world rhythms in a book that allows for both solo and ensemble performance. The use of graphic as well as traditional notation should allow both the novice and the experienced performer to benefit from these materials. Alfred Publishing is to be commended for bringing together the talents of a world percussion artist with those of a world percussion educator to make our understanding of world percussion more enlightened and informed.

Dr. Willis Rapp
Kutztown University of Pennsylvania

introduction

About the Book

Drum Circle: A Guide to World Percussion presents techniques, tones, history and rhythms for percussion instruments found on four continents. The goal of this text is to stimulate the individual's vocabulary with key, culturally specific rhythms and an overall view of their histories and traditional styles. Serving as an introduction to the selected instruments, this book provides an overview of many that have gained notoriety in recent years. Exhaustive study of each instrument will require reference to other instrument-specific texts.

Because different instruments will sometimes share similar techniques, the chapters group similar instruments together into one family regardless of culture. Any instrument within a family may be used interchangeably within the drumming ensemble.

A review of holding and tuning techniques of each drum prepares the player for performance exercises. Technical elements necessary for correct performance on each instrument are discussed, followed by rhythms and their interpretation within the drumming ensemble.

The rhythms and exercises in this book are illustrated in two forms: traditional music notation and time unit box notation. Additionally, traditional syllables are used whenever possible to describe the tones for each instrument. Please note that each drum uses its own set of syllables, and that the number and meaning of the syllables can vary from drum to drum. Please be careful to associate the correct syllables with the correct instrument.

This book is for all music teachers, social studies teachers and drum enthusiasts to use as a tool to build and create world percussion ensembles from a tradition of culturally specific rhythms. It is also for the individual drummer, to bring new ideas into drum circles, community groups, bands of all styles, and wherever drumming can be used to uplift the human spirit and mind.

Understanding Traditional Rhythmic Culture

Staying true to a cultural rhythm is what is referred to as "respecting rhythm traditions." This could include traditions of rhythmic structure, playing technique, preparation before playing, or even the playing environment and who will play the drums.

This book is designed as a means for drum enthusiasts of all levels and ages to gain understanding of where and how culturally specific drumming has influenced the world of modern music. The student can then take culturally specific rhythms and substitute any instrument for performance, much like the modern percussionist. Using traditional rhythmic structures as a basis will empower students to create their own rhythms while learning the traditions of the world's drumming culture. Now, the beat of the world is at your fingertips.

We have been part of a rhythmic evolution that embraces the rhythms of the world. The human race is becoming more culturally diverse and music expresses this. It is only natural for rhythms to cross-pollinate between cultures, creating new versions of what had been. The contribution of our drum culture to the world's rhythms parallels the contributions of drummers from all corners of the earth to this continuous evolution of drumming. The master drummers share the rhythmic knowledge with their communities, and together they create rhythms in a circle of drums where **everyone's a drummer**.

Have Fun Counting Rhythm

Counting rhythm is very important when first studying any style of drumming. A steady pulse is necessary, and using a metronome whenever possible will help develop your inner pulse. We each have a heart that beats a rhythm of life 24/7. Rhythm is inside **everyone**! This book will help you learn to express that inner rhythm on a drum by developing your rhythmic vocabulary while you explore your own creativity.

1. Choose a rhythm from any of the chapters. Start with a slow, steady pulse, counting either eighth notes or sixteenth notes out loud (1 & 2 & 3 & 4 and so on).

2. Before playing the drums, clap the rhythm pattern while counting. Try to memorize the rhythm.

3. Tap your foot to the shaded note area of the time unit box.

4. When comfortable, combine the tap while playing the rhythm.

5. Identify sticking of hand or finger strokes pertaining to the instrument.

6. Remember to take a breath and relax your body.

7. Have fun time between study time, and just play your own groove.

acknowledgements

Chalo Eduardo

Rhythms played for centuries have passed down through the generations by way of aural traditions. Thanks to the many dedicated, professional drummers who have studied specific rhythmic traditions, these rhythms have just recently been written down and documented. It is with the greatest respect to all my peers and the world's family of drummers that I contribute to this natural process by writing this book.

Special thanks: To Alfred Publishing and Mr. Dave Black, for their foresight and perpetuation of hand drumming and world percussion. "Mille grazie" Remo Inc., for the great drums. To my fellow drummers, your influences have inspired me throughout the years. To my co-writer, Frank Kumor, your enthusiasm and talent for drumming are immeasurable. To my Brazilian family and friends, "muito obrigado" for your gift of life in the music, dance and drumming that have lifted my spirit for over 30 years. Special thanks to my wife, Norma, for support and understanding, and to my Mom and Dad who gave me life, love, and support to keep doing what I truly love to do: Drum! And I thank the Lord for a wonderful gift.

Frank Kumor

I would like to take this opportunity to thank the people without whom this project would not have been possible. I will be forever indebted to my wife, Jane Hagness, and my parents, Frank and Roseann Kumor, for their ceaseless love, support and patience, which gives me the strength to continually reach higher. The teachers who have ignited my desire to learn and create will be forever part of my music and work, with particular thanks to Will Rapp and Jim Campbell.

The community, or more accurately, family of drummers around the world is inspirational within itself. This family, regardless of culture, is always eager to share its music with new and old members alike. Leon Mobley, Paulo Mattioli, Randy Crafton, Glen Velez and George Jacob stand out as people who have taught and inspired me with their kindness, wisdom and willingness to share their gifts.

As the world gets smaller and more accessible, the influence of the world's cultures gets larger. I wish to thank all the drummers who have in some way contributed through their influence. It has been a pleasure and education to work with Chalo Eduardo, without whom this book certainly could not have been completed. In addition, I would like to express my thanks and admiration to Remo Belli for manufacturing outstanding instruments and making them available to us and the world. Finally, I extend my gratitude to Dave Black and the staff at Alfred Publishing Company for their help in making this book come alive.

chapter one:

CONGA, TIMBAU, DJEMBE, DOUMBEK

Conga

The *conga* (KON-ga) drums are of Congolese origin, and were brought to Cuba during the African slave trades. The influence of these drums marked the beginning of what is now called Afro-Cuban drumming. "Congas" is a collective noun referring to the trio of drums named *quinto* (KEEN-toe), *conga* and *tumba*, varying in size from smallest to largest, respectively. A skilled player of the congas is called a *conguero*. In popular music, the conga drums are the most-used hand drums from the world's music culture. From traditional Cuban rumba to American disco, the conga drum has evolved into an instrument for all styles of music.

Within the performing ensemble, the congas span the upper- to lower-middle (alto-tenor) voice range. The congas are a timing instrument as well as a solo instrument. In a traditional Cuban drum ensemble, each drum plays a rhythmic role: The quinto is the solo drum; the conga, also called the *tres glopes* (TRAYS GLOW-pay) or *segundo* (se-GOON-doe), is the tenor; the tumba, also called the *tumbadora* or *salidor*, maintains the bass pattern. Three individual drummers play these drums, with one drum each. In modern music, rhythmic patterns are performed by one conguero playing two, three or more drums.

Tuning

In the traditional three-drum conga set, the tuning of the drums can vary and is dependent upon the music and style. The following tuning notes fall in the range of those most commonly used: Quinto tuned to D5, conga tuned to C5, tumba tuned to G4. If a fourth drum were used, the tumba would be tuned to F4.

Playing Position

Many contemporary players use stands that hold single or multiple drums and play in a standing position. Traditionally, however, the conguero plays the drums while seated on the edge of an armless chair, small stool or drum throne. The drum is positioned between the conguero's legs and held with the knees. The drum is slightly angled to one side and secured with the feet. (Some congas with glossy finish slip from between the legs very easily; this may be remedied by the use of a drum strap. Wrap the strap around your waste and snap the hooks onto the tension rods.) If multiple drums are used, one drum is held as described, the conga is placed to the performer's dominant side, and the tumba is placed to the performer's weak side. Also popular is setting the drums in an inverted "V" shape with the quinto, conga and tumba on the dominant side of the seated player.

Performance Technique

Six tones are produced on the conga: The *bass tone*, *open tone*, *slap tone* (or *open slap*), *muffled tone* (or *mute tone*), *palm tone*, and *tap* (*closed slap* or *tapado*). When executing the open and slap tones, the hand must be allowed to rebound naturally. The wrist and shoulders should be relaxed, and care taken to avoid any quick jerking motions. As with all hand drums, it is very important to achieve the differences between tones. Work to improve the quality of each distinctive tone. The greater the difference in tones, the greater the level of the player.

Technical Checklist

1. Form a right angle or a "V" shape with the tips of the index fingers for the set position.

2. You should always keep your hands relaxed. If the fingertips begin to point upward, then the hand is too tense. The hand position should feel natural.

3. You should keep the fingers together for closed hand positions. Avoid open hand positions.

4. Strokes should use the wrist and forearm. In the set position, the elbows should be extended away from the body. In the up position, the elbows should be against the body.

The three principle tones produced on the conga drums are the bass tone, open tone and slap tone. The three supporting tones are the palm tone, tap and mute tone. All but the bass strokes are executed by flexing the wrists.

Open Tone

Your wrists and shoulders should be relaxed when playing. Place the hands on the drum to form a "V" shape with the knuckles (where the fingers join to the palm) at the *bearing edge*, keeping thumbs away from the rim. On the upstroke, flex the wrist so that the palm faces out; on the downstroke, strike the drum rolling the hand from palm to fingertips. Do not hit the palm directly on the bone.

Slap Tone

The slap stroke is similar to the open tone. The difference occurs at the moment of impact: When striking the drum, the fingers should grab the drumhead using a quick, snapping motion. The crucial point of contact should be felt in the fingertips. Hold the hand down on the drumhead for a closed slap, and let the hand rebound for the open slap.

Bass Tone

There are two techniques for producing a bass tone, each using a different part of the hand.

The first is generally referred to as the *bass stroke*, and uses the lower portion of the palm closest to the wrist. To produce this tone, place your hands parallel to each other on the drum while tilting the drum to one side, allowing the bass tone to ring out. Keep the wrists straight, bend the arm at the elbow and strike the center of the drum with the palm of the hand, making sure the fingers are not touching the drumhead.

The second technique is generally referred to as the *palm stroke*, and is produced using a full hand in the center of the drum while slightly flexing the fingers.

Palm Tone

Keeping the hands flat on the drumhead, add a slight pressure at the point where the fingers and palm meet. The Afro-Cuban rocking motion called *tapado* (described below) is created by playing a tap in this position by slightly raising the fingers.

Tap Stroke

This stroke is used as a filler stroke, tapping the drum with the fingers between other tones. Using the open tone hand position (or "V" position), keep the fingers on the drum so they curve naturally, with the tips resting on the drumhead. This position creates a slight gap between the drum and the arched fingers.

A technique characteristic of the Afro-Cuban style of drumming involves the use of the palm and tap strokes, called *tapado*. Place the hand in the middle of the drumhead, and combine the palm and tap in one rocking motion while playing a slap tone. Many rhythms like the *tumbao* for mambo or the 6/8 *bembe* use this technique. See exercise for congas.

Mute Tone

This tone is played the same as the open tone with only one difference: The mute tone is played with the finger by striking flat on the drum and pressing into the drumhead, preventing the tone from ringing out.

Always allow the hand to rebound naturally, and avoid any quick, jerking motions. Remember that the primary goal is to produce three distinctly different tones. Achieving this marks the difference between a good player and a great player. A helpful technique is to practice in front of a mirror. This will improve your symmetry, enabling you to play even strokes with both hands (see the following exercises).

Exercises and Traditional Rhythms

Exercise 1 🎵 **Track 1**

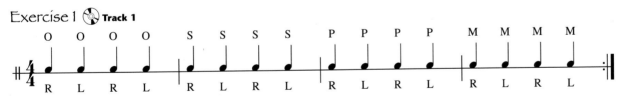

8th-note count	1	+	2	+	3	+	4	+	1	+	2	+	3	+	4	+
Exercise 1	O	O	O	O	S	S	S	S	P	P	P	P	M	M	M	M
Sticking	R	L	R	L	R	L	R	L	R	L	R	L	R	L	R	L
16th note count	1	e	+	a	2	e	+	a	3	e	+	a	4	e	+	a

Exercise 2 🎵 **Track 2**

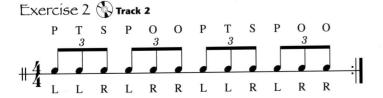

8th-note count	1	+	2	+	3	+	1	+	2	+	3	+
Exercise 2	P	T	S	P	O	O	P	T	S	P	O	O
Sticking	L	L	R	L	R	R	L	L	R	L	R	R
16th-note count	1	e	a	2	e	a	3	e	a	4	e	a

Rhythm 🔘 **Track 3**

♩ = 100

8th-note count	1	+	2	+	3	+	4	+	1	+	2	+	3	+	4	+
Rhythm	S	S	P		S	**O**	S	**O**		S	**O**		S	**O**	S	
Sticking	R	L	R		L	R	L	R		L	R		L	R	L	
16th-note count	1	e	+	a	2	e	+	a	3	e	+	a	4	e	+	a

Key

O = Open tone
S = Slap tone
P = Palm
M = Mute tone
O = Low drum
R = Right hand
L = Left hand

Timbau

The *timbau* (CHIM-bow) comes from Brazil, originating from the Bantu in Africa, and is a cousin of the *ashiko* from West Africa. The drum is conical in shape and tuned high in pitch, with a thin, plastic drumhead. It has a wide tonal range. This drum came to prominence in Brazil in the 1980s with the African influence of the Northern State of Salvador, Bahia. During the Bahian *Carnaval*, the timbau is played by groups numbering in the hundreds parading the streets, and with groups playing on amplified trucks called *Trio Eletricos*.

Tuning

A very high pitch characterizes the tuning of the timbau. The drumhead should be tensioned using a *cross-tuning* method. Choose any tension rod to begin. The next tension rod to be tightened is the one 180 degrees from the original rod. Divide this distance in half (or as close to half as possible) and continue, following this same pattern. Repeat the sequence until each tension rod has been adjusted. The pitch at each tension rod should be the same, which will insure equal pressure on the drumhead.

Playing Position

Like the surdo drum, the timbau is traditionally played suspended from a strap over the performer's shoulder. It is held to the side or straddled between the player's legs. The timbau can also be played using a single conga stand.

Performance Technique

Striking the center of the drum produces a low, rich bass tone. Striking the rim produces a high pitch much like a timbale rim shot. The technique is similar to that used to play the djembe. Most of the rhythms are played using alternating strokes.

Bass Tone

Without bending the wrist, strike the center of the drumhead with the full hand, producing a full, resonant tone.

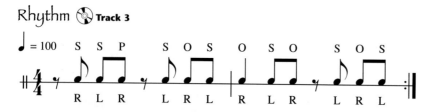

Open Tone

Using a wrist stroke, strike the drum at the bearing edge with the hand. The palm of the hand contacts the edge, allowing the fingers to produce the tone. This stroke is like the muffled tone on the congas, where the hand presses slightly on the drumhead to control the overtones.

Slap Tone

The slap on the timbau is produced with slightly opened fingers, allowing the tone to ring out. Use the same even strokes as you would for the conga or djembe.

Rim Tone

The rim tone is played on the bearing edge of the drum, producing a high pitch. For syllables pertaining to the high tones produced on the timbau, see the following section on the djembe.

Exercises and Traditional Rhythms

Exercise 🔘 **Track 4**

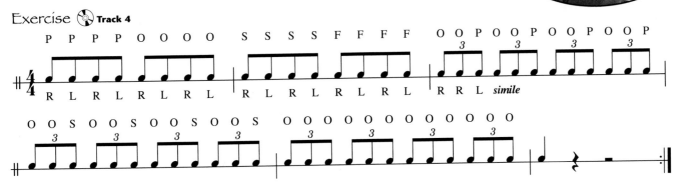

Rhythm 🔘 **Track 5**

♩ = 100

8th-note count	1	+	2	+	3	+	4	+	1	+	2	+	3	+	4	+
Tones	S			S			O	O			S		S		O	O
Sticking	R	L	R	L	R	L	R	L	R	L	R	L	R	L	R	L
16th-note count	1	e	+	a	2	e	+	a	3	e	+	a	4	e	+	a

Key

P = Palm bass tone
O = Open tone
S = Slap tone
F = Fingertips
T = Tap stroke

Variation: Add tap strokes in blank squares.

Djembe

The *djembe* (JEM-bay, also spelled *jembe*) comes from Mali and Guinea in Africa. It can also be found in Senegal, The Ivory Coast and Burkina Faso. It functions either as a lead instrument or as an accompaniment to traditional dances of the region. Construction features the upper portion of the drum, a bowl covered with a single head, connected to the lower, conical-shaped portion at an opening in the bottom of the bowl. The smaller end of the conical segment is joined to the bowl, leaving the larger, flared end at the bottom of the drum. The djembe is often referred to as a "goblet drum" because of its curious shape.

Tuning

The djembe features two different tensioning mechanisms. When using either system, it is important that the counter hoop and the rim of the drumhead remain level at all times. The drumhead should be tight, with a high pitch that allows the performer to hear and produce the characteristic tones of the drum.

The first tuning method is the *rope tensioning* system called the *Mali weave*. The rope runs vertically along the sides of the upper bowl of the drum and fastens to a counter hoop. The counter hoop draws the head down onto the bowl of the drum. The rope is woven, beginning at the bottom of the bowl, and continues upward. Each successive weave increases the tension applied to the head.

The production of instruments in recent years features a tensioning system similar to that of the modern conga drum. This system functions by tightening each tension rod, drawing the head tighter to the drum. Tension should be applied as evenly as possible around the circumference of the drumhead.

Playing Position

Traditionally, the performer stands with the djembe fastened around the waist and the playing surface at waist level. The drum is suspended between the legs of the performer, and the far side of the head is angled slightly downward. The hands should be positioned so the tips of the index fingers form a right angle or "V" shape.

Performance Technique

The djembe can produce three primary tones: a bass tone, a middle tone and a high tone. In the traditional teaching language, each tone is given a separate name depending on whether it is produced by the dominant hand or the weak hand.

The following syllables apply to the dominant hand and the weak hand, respectively.

Bass-tone syllables: *gun* (GOON) and *dun* (DOON)
Middle-tone syllables: *go* (GO) and *do* (DOE)
High-tone syllables: *pa* (PAH) and *ta* (TAH)

Always allow the hand to rebound naturally off the head, which produces a tone of the highest quality. The primary goal is to produce three distinctly different tones. Without these tones, the language of the drum is unclear.

Bass Tones: Gun/Dun

These tones are produced by simply allowing the full hand to make contact with the center of the drum. This technique produces a very deep and resonant tone. The hand should remain relaxed and the wrist should remain straight. Upon impact, the entire hand should contact the head evenly. No part of the hand should contact the drum before another.

Middle Tones: Go/Do

With the hands in the original set position, draw them back while maintaining the original position. Note that the fingertips will no longer be in contact with each other. The stroke execution should be the same as for the gun/dun stroke. The bearing edge of the drum should come across the palm of the hand where the fingers begin, with the thumb positioned so as to avoid striking the drum during the stroke. The tone is produced using only the fingers; however, each finger in its entirety should make contact with the drum. It is important to keep the wrist straight. Do not let it relax around the contour of the bearing edge. The tone produced should be a full sound with limited low and high timbres.

High Tones: Pa/Ta

The pa/ta tones are the highest tones produced on the djembe and are very powerful. They can project over the largest drumming ensembles. The tones are produced by drawing the hands further back in the same manner as for the go/do tones. Note that the hand follows the contour of the bearing edge of the drum. The top two-thirds of the fingers strike the drum, producing a very high-pitched tone. The fingers must remain in the closed position and curve around the drum.

Exercises and Traditional Rhythms

8th-note count	1	+	2	+	3	+	4	+	1	+	2	+	3	+	4	+
Rhythm	Gu				Pt	Gu		Go	Gu			Pt	Gu		Go	
Hands		L	R	L	R	L	R	L	R	L	R	L	R	L	R	L	R
16th-note count	1	e	+	a	2	e	+	a	3	e	+	a	4	e	+	a

Key
Gu = Gun/Dun
Go = Go/Do
Pt = Pa/Ta

Doumbek

The *doumbek* (DOOM-beck) is often described as a "goblet drum" because of its similar shape and size. The drum has many names depending on where you go, among them being *darabukka, darbuka, darabuke* and *derbukka*, to name only a few. The doumbek or its relatives can be found in Egypt, North Africa, Mesopotamia and Arabic countries. Depending on its country of origin, the doumbek is made of wood, ceramic or metal. The drumhead has been made of goatskin, fish skin, ram skin and even dog skin. Many contemporary instruments are made of metal or ceramic with a goatskin or plastic head. In classical Persian music, the darabukka is the primary percussion instrument. It also appears in drum ensembles, accompanying dances or performing traditional ensemble music.[1]

Tuning

Many instruments have heads that are glued or tacked to the drum and are not tunable. If the drum is tunable by chord or any modern tuning devices, the head should be rather tight. This will produce rich, warm and booming bass tones as well as a projecting edge tone. As with other hand drums, be sure that the head remains level.

Playing Position

The doumbek is played in either of two positions.

In the first position, the drum rests across the performer's thigh, secured with the arm. The bottom of the drum is then pointing behind the performer. The weak hand rests on top of the drum's shell while the dominant hand is placed in front of the drum.

The second position cradles the drum between the performer's legs allowing free, symmetrical and unrestricted access to the drum's playing surface.

Performance Technique

The doumbek produces two basic tones: *dun* (DOON) and *tek* (TECK) (or *kah* [KAW], depending on which hand is performing the stroke). The performer should sit with relaxed shoulders and arms. This allows for the arms, wrists and fingers to move efficiently and smoothly. The most important technical issue to remember is that the contrast between the two different tones should be as great as possible.

Bass Tone: Dun

The dun is created in a manner similar to its performance on the djembe or conga. Strike the center of the playing surface with a relaxed hand. The tone should be full and resonant.

[1]Conner, William, Howell, Milfie, Langlois, Tony. "Darabukar" <u>The New Grove Dictionary of Music & Musicians</u> Macmillan Publishers Ltd., New York, 2000 , Volume 3, pp. 526-528

High Tone: Tek/Kah

The tek is produced by striking the drum at the bearing edge using only the upper two-thirds of the fingers. The tone should be very high in pitch and very short in duration. The motion should be relaxed and fluid, not stiff or robotic.

Exercises and Traditional Rhythms

Exercise 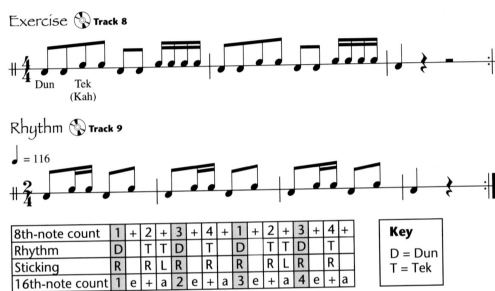 **Track 8**

Dun   Tek
(Kah)

Rhythm **Track 9**

♩ = 116

8th-note count	1	+	2	+	3	+	4	+	1	+	2	+	3	+	4	+
Rhythm	D		T	T	D		T		D		T	T	D		T	
Sticking	R		R	L	R		R		R		R	L	R		R	
16th-note count	1	e	+	a	2	e	+	a	3	e	+	a	4	e	+	a

Key

D = Dun
T = Tek

chapter two:
frame drums

TAMBORIM, TAR, BODHRAN

Frame drums are among the oldest instruments in the percussion family. Evidence of the frame drum has been observed in the carvings and paintings of ancient cultures. The basic design is an instrument with a circular shell approximately two to four inches in depth. The diameter of the drums generally ranges from six to twenty-two inches. The drumhead consists of an animal, fish or reptile skin that is stretched across one side of the drum. Some instruments have skins stretched across both sides of the drum and loose grains or other small materials placed inside. This adds a myriad of sound possibilities to the drum. In many cultures, women were the exclusive artists of frame drum performance.

Tamborim

The *tamborim* (tam-bore-EEM) is a small drum played with a splintered stick called the *baqueta*. This drum is a high voice (soprano) in Brazilian samba ensembles, called *bateria*. The number of tamborim players in a bateria can well exceed 20. In Brazil's Carnaval parade, at least 70 tamborim players is common. Rhythmic accuracy as well as style is important when playing the tamborim; the tamborim section enhances the performance with flashy visuals in which all the players break into synchronized choreography while continuing to play rhythms on the instruments. These visuals not only add to the character of the music, they contribute to the phrasing and feel that is characteristic of the Escola de Samba (samba schools), and Brazilian Carnaval music in Rio de Janeiro. In the tradition of the Escola de Samba, the tamborim plays rhythmic figures outlining the melody of the *samba enredo* (SAM-ba en-HAY-doe), as well as playing key patterns in unison.

Tuning

In the samba school, a very high pitch characterizes the tamborim tuning. Striking the drum with the baqueta produces a very loud, glassy sound. In other styles, the tamborim is tuned lower to any desired pitch within the context of the music, as in the *bossa nova* and *samba cancao*.

Playing Position

The tamborim is held with all four fingers on the inside of the drum and the thumb outside, away from the drumhead. The drumhead should be facing the performer and the open shell should face outward. Hold the baqueta as you would a drumstick, with the index finger and thumb gripping the stick while the other three fingers curve around the handle. The tamborim can also be played with a thin drumstick, producing a warmer sound.

Performance Technique

When using the baqueta, strike the head simultaneously across the full diameter of the drum and the rim, similar to a rudimental rim shot. This technique produces a very loud and projecting tone. When using a stick, strike the drum only on the drumhead. The stroke is a full stroke consisting of a downward motion followed by an upstroke that returns the stick to its originating position. Modifying this basic technique can also incorporate a visual element. When striking the drum on the downstroke, follow through by allowing the stick to pass beyond the playing level of the drum and letting the force of the stroke rotate the drum 180 degrees. The drumhead is now facing the floor. This is immediately followed by an upstroke that contacts the inverted drum, and upon doing so, follows through to return both stick and drum to the original playing position.

Closed or Mute Tones

Closed tones are produced by allowing the fingers to contact the underside of the drumhead while playing on the head with the stick.

Open Tones

Open tones are produced when the drumhead is allowed to vibrate without the interference of extra finger contact.

Note: When playing with the baqueta in the samba enredo style, muting the underside of the drumhead is not practiced. The tone should ring out.

Exercises and Traditional Rhythms

Exercise ⊙ **Track 10**

Tr   Tr   Tr   Tr

Rhythm ⊙ **Track 11**

♩ = 120

Samba Turnaround   Samba Rhythm

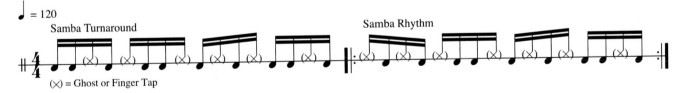

(×) = Ghost or Finger Tap

8th-note count	1	+	2	+	3	+	4	+	1	+	2	+	3	+	4	+
Rhythm		X		X		X	X		X		X		X	X		X
Tones	O		O		O	O			O		O		O	O		O
16th-note count	1	e	+	a	2	e	+	a	3	e	+	a	4	e	+	a

Key
X = Stick striking drumhead
F = Finger holding drum with light taps on back of drumhead
Tr = Turning drum
O = Open tone
+ = Mute tone

Tar

The name of this instrument, *tar*, is derived from two words of the southern Arabic language *Soqotri*, meaning "frame drum" and "round object."[2] The drums can range in size from approximately six to twenty inches in diameter. They appear traditionally throughout the Arabic cultures. The tar is used to accompany dance as well as to serve in ceremonial rites.

Tuning

Because the head is most commonly tacked or woven onto the drum, the tar is usually not tunable; however, some instruments are tunable and these drums should be evenly tensioned and moderately tight.

Playing Position

The drum is cradled in the palm of the weak hand and stabilized by the thumb, which sits on the inside of the shell (back). The fingers should curve around the front of the drum in position to play the strokes (front). The thumb of the strong hand is placed about one-third from the bottom of the shell. This becomes a pivot point around which the hand rotates to strike the drum.

Performance Technique

It is possible to produce a great number of sounds on a tar. Four of the primary strokes are the *full tone*, *edge tone*, the *snap* and *scratch*.

Full Tone: Dun

The full tone is produced by striking the drum with a full, flat finger of the dominant hand, one-third to one-half the distance between the edge and center of the drum. The lead finger used for executing rhythms is the fourth finger, also known as the ring finger. Upon impact, the finger should be flat against the head. The stroke is a rotation of the hand, which pivots around the point where the thumb rests against the shell. The stroke must be relaxed and quick so that the finger rebounds off the drum. Without proper relaxation and speed, the hand will immediately muffle the tone, producing a dull, dry sound. The goal is to produce a full, resonant tone.

Edge Tone: Tak

The edge tone is produced using the same technique as the open tone; however, the playing area is right against the bearing edge of the drum. This stroke can be performed using all fingers. It is recommended that each finger individually isolate the stroke before combinations are practiced. Again, it is important to rebound off the stroke quickly in order to produce the most resonant tone.

[2]Poché, Christian. "Tar" The New Grove Dictionary of Musical Instruments Macmillan Publishers Ltd., New York, 1984 , Volume 3, pp. 526-528

Snap

The snap stroke is unique to the frame drum family. It functions as an accented edge tone. This tone is produced by snapping the fingers. The drum shell should be placed against the base of the thumb so that the snapped finger hits the drum instead of the thumb, producing a sharp, accented tone.

Scratch

Scratching is performed by curving the hand so that only the fingertips touch the drum. Moving the hand in a back-and-forth motion across the surface of the head creates the scratching tone, which, in addition to its unique timbre, also has length.

Exercises and Traditional Rhythms

Exercise 🎧 **Track 12**

Dun   Tak   S = Scratch   Snap

Rhythm 🎧 **Track 13**

♩ = 95

8th-note count	1	+	2	+	3	+	4	+	1	+	2	+	3	+	4	+
Exercise	D			T	T		T	T	D		D		T	T	T	T
Call to Dance	R		R	L		L	R		R		R		R	L	R	L
16th-note count	1	e	+	a	2	e	+	a	3	e	+	a	4	e	+	a

Key

D = Dun
T = Tak

- The "tak" tones can be substituted with slides or scrapes as demonstrated on the recording.

Bodhran

The *bodhran* (BOW-rahn), usually 18 to 22 inches in diameter, is similar to the tar in its construction. Its name is derived from *bodhar,* which means "deaf" or "dull-sounding."[3] One difference is the added feature of one or two crossing dowels set inside the frame of the drum. This provides a handle for the drum and positions the performer's hand so the backside of the head may be manipulated. Also, unlike the tar, the bodhran is traditionally played with a two-headed stick called the *cipin* (SIP-in) or *tipper,* although the hand is used in some regions of Ireland. The bodhran is used to accompany traditional songs and dances of Ireland.

Tuning

Generally, the bodhran features a skin that is tacked to the shell and is not tunable; however, more recently produced instruments can feature specialized tuning mechanisms. In regard to tunable instruments, the tension should be even at all tension points to produce a pitch that is warm and resonant. Tuning too tight will produce a thin sound and too low will not produce enough resonance. Experiment with your drum and find the best tension level for the instrument.

Playing Position

A seated playing position has evolved as the position of choice among contemporary bodhran players. The drum itself is held by the inside cross bars with the weak hand. The shell of the drum can rest on the forearm. The cipin is held at the midpoint in the dominant hand. The thumb and index finger grip the cipin like a pencil using the "point" of the pencil as the primary side, which performs or leads the rhythms.

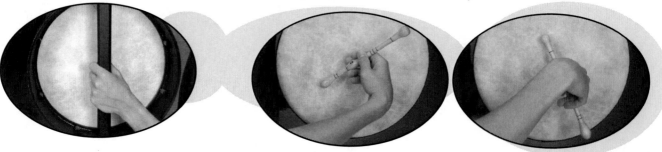

Performance Technique

There are three basic types of strokes performed on the bodhran: the *downstroke, upstroke* and *roll.* The playing hand should be bent slightly at the wrist to place the cipin in the proper playing position. The correct playing area for downstrokes is halfway between the center of the drum and the performer's body. The correct playing area for upstrokes is between the center of the drum and bottom of the drum. These strokes, individually and in combination, create energetic and intricate rhythms strong enough to provide a solid foundation for the drumming ensemble, and powerful enough for dynamic solos.

[3] Ó Suilleabháin, Michael. "Bodhran" <u>The New Grove Dictionary of Musical Instruments</u> Macmillan Publishers Ltd., New York, 1984 , Volume 1, pp. 243-244

chapter two: frame drums

Downstroke

The downstroke is the primary leading stroke for the performance of rhythms on the bodhran. It is performed using a sweeping, downward motion and a very relaxed grip. Too much finger tension will result in an inflexible wrist. Be sure to maintain the bent wrist position. The tone should be a full resonant sound. At the completion of the downstroke, the hand is in position to play the upstroke.

Upstroke

The upstroke is performed in exactly the opposite manner as the downstroke. The playing end of the cipin is swung back toward the head, producing the upstroke tone. The upstroke follows the downstroke.

Roll

The back of the cipin on the follow through of the downstroke produces the roll. Essentially, this stroke produces a double downstroke, which is similar to a double bounce in rudimental drumming.

Exercises and Traditional Rhythms

Exercise **Track 14**

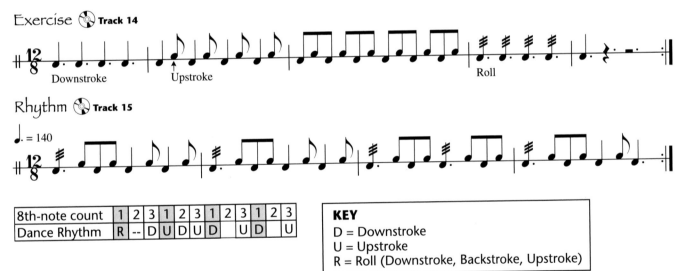

Rhythm **Track 15**

8th-note count	1	2	3	1	2	3	1	2	3	1	2	3
Dance Rhythm	R	--	D	U	D	U	D		U	D		U

KEY

D = Downstroke
U = Upstroke
R = Roll (Downstroke, Backstroke, Upstroke)

chapter three:
frame drums with jingles

PANDEIRO, RIQQ, TAMBOURINE

Frame drums with jingles are found in cultures around the world. They are similar to the standard frame drum in construction; however, slits are made along the circumference of the drum shell and disks of metal or bells are set into the slots. The addition of jingles adds a timbral element to the sound of the instrument. The size of these drums generally ranges from six to fourteen inches.

Pandeiro

The *pandeiro* (pawn-DAY-ru) is of Brazilian origin. It is similar to the Western tambourine, but has a set of three jingles per slot. One flat jingle is placed between two domed jingles. Multiple sets fill the entire circumference of the drum. A tunable, single drumhead of animal skin or plastic completes the construction of the drum. The various styles of Brazilian music use various sizes of pandeiros that range from 10 to 14 inches in diameter. Tuning depends upon the size of the instrument and the style of music being performed. In performance, the pandeiro is used similarly to the tamborim in that it serves both a rhythmic and visual function. Rhythmically, the pandeiro creates a steady pulse of sixteenth notes. Within the steady rhythmic pattern, the combination of the different tones creates the characteristic phrasing associated with the samba style. Visually, the pandeiro players use the instrument to juggle, spin and execute synchronized choreography among the players and dancers in the Carnaval parade. The combination of these visual and technical elements contributes to the characteristic style and feel of the music.

Tuning

In Brazil, the musical style would determine the pandeiro's tuning. In the Escola de Samba or *pagode* styles (see "Tan-Tan"), a 12-inch pandeiro is generally tuned to a high pitch. In the traditional music of Chorinhos, a 10-inch or 11-inch pandeiro is tuned to a low pitch, which simulates a surdo. In general, tuning the pandeiro to C5 (medium tension) is a good starting point.

Playing Position

Hold the pandeiro in the weak hand between the space of any two jingles, with the fingers inside the drum and the thumb on the rim. The drum should be held out in front of the body at a slight angle to provide a comfortable playing position for the strong hand.

Performance Technique

Four strokes and two tones comprise the basic performance techniques on the pandeiro. In addition, the jingles can be activated by rotating the wrist of the weak hand. Always maintain contact with the drumhead using one part of the strong hand.

Slap

The slap tone is produced by striking the center of the drum with the full hand, using a snapping stroke with fingers slightly apart. This produces a sound that is very loud, short and high in pitch. This stroke is similar to that used on the hand drums (see "Chapter One").

Thumb Stroke

The full length of the thumb strikes the drumhead, producing an open or closed tone.

Thumb Roll (See "Tambourine")

Fingertip Stroke

The tip stroke is performed using only the tips of the fingers on the dominant hand. This stroke comes between the thumb stroke and the heel stroke within the sixteenth-note rhythm.

Heel Stroke

The heel is the lower part of the palm, just before the wrist. This stroke is easily executed by using the heel of the hand to strike the pandeiro.

Open Tone

The open tones are produced when the head is allowed to vibrate freely after a stroke. This is achieved by keeping the fingers of the weak hand clear from the back of the drumhead.

Closed Tone

The closed tone is achieved by pressing the fingers of the weak hand into the back of the drumhead, producing a short, muffled tone.

The following symbols are used to indicate the intended strokes: O=Open thumb, +=Closed thumb, S=Slap, H=Heel, F=Fingertips.

Exercises and Traditional Rhythms

Exercise 🔊 **Track 16**

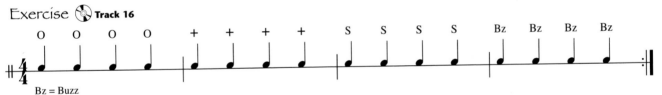

Bz = Buzz

Rhythm 🔊 **Track 17**

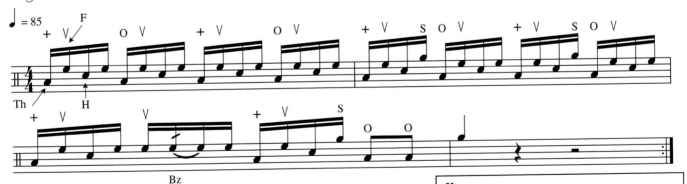

Bz

8th-note count	1	+	2	+	3	+	4	+	1	+	2	+	3	+	4	+
Accent	X	V		X	X	V			X	X	V		X	X	V		X
Tones	+	+	+	+	O	O	O	O	+	+	+	+	O	O	O	O
Strokes	Th	F	H	F	Th	F		H	F	Th	F	H	F	Th	F	H	F
16th-note count	1	e	+	a	2	e	+	a	3	e	+	a	4	e	+	a

Key

O = Open tone with thumb
+ = Mute tone: Opposite hand inside of drum while striking open with thumb
F = Fingertips
H = Heel of hand
Th = Thumb
Bz = Buzz roll
V = Lift slightly
⌣ = Tie duration of beats
S = Slap

Riqq

The *riqq* (RICK) features jingles that are larger than those of the pandeiro and set in two parallel rows. Found in Egypt, Iraq, Lebanon, Libya, Palestine, Syria and others, this instrument, like its relatives, is used to accompany traditional dance, song and ceremonial music. The name, used since the nineteenth century, comes from three words meaning "thin," "to be a slave" and "drum." Other names, such as *tar* or *duff*, can also refer to this instrument.[4] The riqq traditionally can be played in one or a combination of three different playing positions. This book only focuses on the primary position and the strokes necessary to produce the characteristic tones on the instrument.

Playing Position

The riqq is held in the weak hand. The position of the instrument is critical for accurate technical execution. The riqq should rest in the hand with the thumb positioned over the first row of jingles and resting on the second row of jingles. This contact with the second pair of jingles provides control over the tones produced on that jingle. The instrument should be angled so that the top of the riqq leans slightly forward. This position produces a short, dry tone from the jingles. Tones are produced on the head as well as on the jingles of the instrument.

Performance Technique

As with many instruments, the number of possible sounds is limited to one's imagination; however, there are five traditional tones: *tik* (TICK), *dun* (DOON), *tak* (TOCK), *kah* (KAW) and the *side hit*.

Tik

Tik is produced by playing on the jingle, which is positioned at the bottom of the instrument. The ring finger of each hand can play on this jingle to produce quick rhythmic figures. The middle and index fingers of the strong hand can also be included to improve rhythmic clarity in the execution of very fast ornamental figures. The fingers should remain straight to avoid clawing at the jingles.

Dun

Dun is the bass tone on the riqq. It is produced using the index finger of the strong hand to strike the drum slightly off-center, making sure that the finger completely contacts the drumhead. The hand should move in a rotating motion toward and away from the drum. Too little contact will produce a shallow, non-projecting tone. The tone should be resonant and deep.

Tak

Tak is a high-pitched tone produced by striking the drum at the edge using the middle finger of each hand. Be certain to keep the ring finger of each hand off the drum near the jingle to give the middle fingers enough room to easily contact the drum.

[4]Poché, Christian. "Riqq" The New Grove Dictionary of Musical Instruments, Macmillan Publishers Ltd., New York, 1984 , Volume 3, pp. 250-251

Kah

Kah is a mute stroke that can be played using one or a combination of three variations.

The basic stroke is played with the fingertips of the strong hand. All four fingers push into the center of the drumhead. The weak hand can assist this stroke by letting the drum fall forward and the strong hand can then push the drum back up to its playing position. The tone is a soft, muffled tone, not a slap.

The second variation is the more commonly played stroke, which does resemble the slap of a conga. This stroke is played using the fingertips of the strong hand. The tone is a "pop" or a "slap" sound that is louder than the muffled kah.

The third variation is similar to the first muffled tone; however, using a quick rotation of the wrist, the thumb is allowed to scrape the surface of the drum, creating a "flam" effect. (A *flam* is a traditional rudimental drum stroke where one ornamental stroke strikes the drum slightly before the principal stroke.)

Side Hit

The side hit is a jingle effect created by bringing the riqq to a position perpendicular to the floor. This position allows the jingles freedom to shake without gravity working against them. Strike the instrument on the shell using the palm of the hand. This technique produces a resonant tone consisting of all the jingles vibrating in combination with the sympathetic vibration of the drumhead.

Exercises and Traditional Rhythms

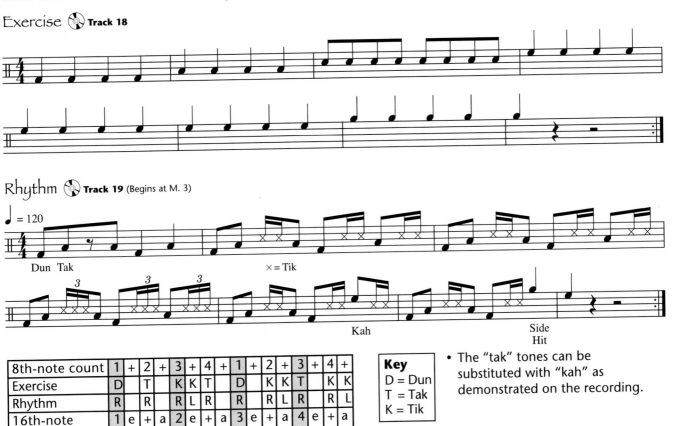

Exercise 🔊 Track 18

Rhythm 🔊 Track 19 (Begins at M. 3)

♩ = 120

Dun Tak   × = Tik

Kah   Side Hit

8th-note count	1	+	2	+	3	+	4	+	1	+	2	+	3	+	4	+
Exercise	D		T			K	K	T	D			K	K	T		K	K
Rhythm	R		R		R	L	R		R		R	L	R		R	L
16th-note count	1	e	+	a	2	e	+	a	3	e	+	a	4	e	+	a

Key
D = Dun
T = Tak
K = Tik

• The "tak" tones can be substituted with "kah" as demonstrated on the recording.

Tambourine

The *tambourine* is easily one of the most widely used percussion instruments for all styles of music and in music programs for all ages. Of European descent, it is derived from its ancient relative, the *timbral* of Assyria and Egypt. Forms of the instrument have been found in China and central Asia (Diere), India (Daph), Peru (Chil Chil) and Greenland (Aelyau). It is used as an accompaniment to dance and in Roman Bacchic rites.

The Hebrew equivalent is named the *tof*. The modern instrument is fundamental to the classical percussionist's training and performance. It has been commonly used as a color or style element in orchestral music since the nineteenth century, and continues to be scored in band and small ensemble compositions as well as classical and popular music.[5]

Tuning

Most classical tambourines are available with a tunable drumhead. In popular music, it is commonly played without a drumhead.

Playing Position

Hold the tambourine vertically in one hand, out in front of the body without bending the wrist. Using the dominant hand, activate the jingles with an even, back-and-forth motion.

Performance Technique

The palm of the weak hand is opened and struck with the tambourine one quarter-inch above the wrist. The tambourine is an extremely versatile instrument that can also utilize most frame drum techniques.

Multiple tones are possible on tambourines with a drumhead, but are more limited on those without a drumhead. Some common tones include the *slap, open tone, side hit* and *edge tone*, among others. The jingle tones vary from drum to drum. Choose the sound that fits your musical needs.

Thumb Roll

This stroke is a technique commonly used in orchestral performance and can be employed by all frame drums. Friction is used to create a seamless roll by pushing the thumb across the drumhead. The instrument is held in the weak hand. Keeping the thumb relaxed but straight, the tip of the thumb pushes around the circumference of the drum. This results in a series of tiny bounces caused by the friction on the drumhead. Various materials such as bee's wax, sandpaper and rosin are applied to natural skin heads, making this technique quick and easy. This stroke can prove to be slightly more difficult on tambourines with synthetic drumheads due to the smoothness and consistency of the drumhead.

Exercises and Traditional Rhythms

[5]Blades, James. Percussion Instruments and Their History, Faber and Faber Ltd., London, 1974

Rhythm ♩ = 85

🔘 Track 20

8th-note count	1	+	2	+	3	+	4	+	1	+	2	+	3	+	4	+
Direction	←	→	←	→	←	→	←	→	←	→	←	→	←	→	←	→
Tones					S		F						S			
16th-note count	1	e	+	a	2	e	+	a	3	e	+	a	4	e	+	a

Key

← → = Tambourine movement
P = Tambourine strikes palm
S = Slap tone
F = Tambourine strikes fingers

chapter four: bass drums

SURDO, DJUN DJUN, TAN-TAN

Bass drums are essentially the heartbeat of the drumming ensemble. Although they typically play less intricate patterns, they mark the significant beats, creating the unique rhythm. Whether it is a *nanigo* or a *samba*, the rhythm of the bass drums define the style.

Surdo

The *surdo* (SOOR-doe) is a double-headed bass drum found in Brazil. The word surdo means "deaf." It is the heartbeat of the samba rhythm section called the *bateria*. The surdo provides the bass voice in the Brazilian percussion ensemble as its deep, relatively pitched tones establish the foundation upon which the rhythms are layered by the remaining ensemble instruments. Traditionally, the surdo comes in three sizes, called (from largest to smallest) *marcacao* (mar-kaw-SOUN), *resposta* (hes-POE-sta) and *cortador* (core-tah-DOOR). It is played using a medium-hard mallet that is wrapped with foam and covered with a cloth material. Like other Brazilian instruments, the surdo is played with a great deal of rhythmic accuracy, coupled with visual enhancements.

Tuning

There are two types of tuning systems. One is the *single side* tuning system, featuring a mechanism by which each rod is connected to both the top and bottom counter hoops. This tunes the bottom and top heads simultaneously. The top side generally has the tuning lugs where you can use the *cross-tuning system* or tune right to left and vice versa. The second type features a double tension system, where each head is tuned independently with a drum key. This allows for more accurate tuning; however, it is more difficult to tune while parading.

Playing Position

Traditionally, the surdo is held with a single strap over the shoulder and is played while parading. The strap should be over the shoulder of the hand that holds the mallet. Surdos are also played in a stationary position, using a stand or legs that are attached to the shell. This will enable a player to use more then one drum at a time, effectively playing multiple parts as well as simultaneously playing additional instruments like the ganza or tamborim.

Performance Technique

The surdo can be played in traditional and non-traditional environments. You can play the surdo using two mallets as is done in Salvador, Bahia, or a single mallet and bare hand as in the *Carioca* style of Rio de Janeiro.

Open Tone

Strike the surdo with the mallet just off-center. This area of the drum produces the richest tone.

Muffle Tone

Place the opposite hand on the drumhead to eliminate the resonance, and strike the drum just off-center.

Rim Tone

Strike the rim of the drum with the shaft of the mallet.

Exercises and Traditional Rhythms

Rhythm ⊙ **Track 21**

♩ = 100

× = Strike the Rim

8th-note count	4	+	1	+	2	+	3	+	4	+	1	+	2	+	3	+	4	+
Tones	O	T	+		X	T	O		X	T	+		X	T	O		X	T
Sticking	R	L	R		R	L	R		R	L	R		R	L	R		R	L
16th-note count	+	a	1	e	+	a	2	e	+	a	3	e	+	a	4	e	+	a

Key
O = Open tone
+ = Mute tone
T = Hand tap (keep hand on drumhead for mute tone, lift off for open tone)
X = Stick strikes rim
M = Muffled tone

Note: Surdo rhythm starts with an open tone pick-up beat.

Djun Djun

The *djun djun* (JOON JOON, also spelled *dun dun*) is a double-headed bass drum indigenous to Africa. This instrument is the bass voice in many types of African drum ensembles and is usually seen with a bell mounted on the side of the drum shell. Combinations of drum and bell patterns are played to form the foundation of the music. The African drum ensemble is used to accompany traditional dance and rituals. The djun djun comes in varying sizes that can be combined to form a melodic and rhythmic musical structure.

Tuning

Although the djun djun is a bass voice in the drum ensemble, the head tuning is fairly tight. It is important to keep consistent tension all around the circumference of the drumhead. Like many traditional instruments, the djun djun originally used a *rope tensioning* system. A single rope, woven around the counter hoops, draws the heads together. This system has been replaced on some instruments by modern tuning devices such as tension rods and claw hooks. Standard tension rods and claw hooks, similar to those used on a modern bass drum, are adjusted with a drum key to tighten or loosen the drumhead.

Both heads of the drum should be as close to the same pitch as possible. The heads should be tight, so that when playing the instrument, there is a strong sense of rebound off the head. The pitch should be relative to the size of the drum; the largest drum should be lowest in pitch, and the smallest drum should be highest in pitch. The smallest djun djun will actually sound fairly high in pitch; however, within the drumming ensemble, this pitch will fall in the tenor range. If the drum is tuned too tightly, the low tones will be lost. A balance among the upper overtones and the lower overtones will yield a full, resonant sound that will project clearly over the ensemble.

Playing Position

On the floor or ground, the djun djun can be laid on its side with the heads of the drum facing to the right and left of the seated performer. Some new instruments have added legs that are fastened to the shell of the drum. These legs can position the drum vertically with one head facing up and one facing down. This drum placement allows the performer to perform while standing rather than sitting.

Performance Technique

The djun djun is played with one hand using a stick or wrapped mallet. A bass drum mallet with a medium-hard beater is an ideal implement. The drum is struck slightly off-center to produce the best tone. All strokes should move in a straight line to and from the head. Any circular or angular stick movement should be avoided, as this is a very inefficient stroke and can promote wrist injury. Dynamic or volume control is achieved by larger or smaller strokes. To increase volume, the mallet should travel a greater distance from the head; conversely, a softer dynamic would require a decreased distance that the mallet travels from the head. For example, a *piano* or soft dynamic might require a three-inch drum stroke, and a *forte* or loud dynamic would require a nine-inch drum stroke.

The two principle strokes used in djun djun performance are *open tones* and *closed tones*. Performing these tones individually and in combination with other djun djun parts can create intricate rhythmic patterns to serve as the foundation for a composition.

Open Tone

The open tone is performed by striking the drum and allowing the mallet to immediately and naturally rebound off the surface of the head. This stroke yields the characteristic tone of the drum.

Closed Tone

The closed tone is performed like the open stroke with one exception: Instead of allowing the mallet to rebound naturally, it is pressed into the drumhead, producing a very short, dry and muffled tone.

When the djun djun is equipped with an attached bell, this instrument is played with whichever hand is not already playing the djun djun. The bell is attached to the side of the drum and played with a stick.

Exercises and Traditional Rhythms

Exercise Track 22

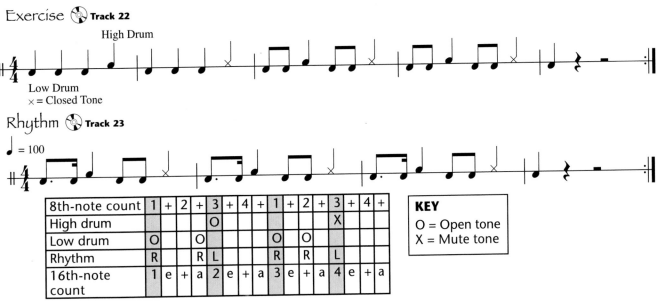

Rhythm Track 23

♩ = 100

8th-note count	1	+	2	+	3	+	4	+	1	+	2	+	3	+	4	+	KEY
High drum					O								X				O = Open tone
Low drum	O				O				O		O						X = Mute tone
Rhythm	R				R	L			R		R		L				
16th-note count	1	e	+	a	2	e	+	a	3	e	+	a	4	e	+	a	

Tan-Tan

The *tan-tan* (TAHN-TAHN) is a tubular-shaped drum that uses a single vinyl drumhead and produces a very low bass tone. The tan-tan serves as a bass drum accompaniment for the samba musical groups called *pagode*. The pagode comes from an older style of samba music called *samba de roda* and *partito alto*. It is arguably one of the most popular styles of samba in Brazil since the 1970s. The ensemble can be composed of a *cavaquinho* (kah-vah-KEEN-oh), *repique de mao* (he-PEEK-ee de mow), tamborim, *agogo*, *cuica* and pandeiro. The ensemble dynamics enable the composers to try out possible songs while singing, and still be heard over the drums. They do this before the Carnaval parade, where there will be a bateria of 300 drummers.

Tuning

Tuned much like the surdo, the tan-tan has two sizes, a 14-inch diameter that is pitched low and a 12-inch, which is pitched higher. The unique quality of this drum is that it uses a vinyl drumhead that eliminates all the high overtones to produce a pure bass sound.

Playing Position

The tan-tan can be played standing with the use of a strap over the neck and shoulder to hold the drum in position. The drum is held in a horizontal position, enabling access to the drumhead and shell. Advanced players can play sitting down, placing the tan-tan on the floor under their legs or across the lap. If there are no surdos, the tan-tan may be played with a mallet and held like the surdo.

Performance Technique

The tan-tan is played by one hand striking the drumhead while the other hand plays on the shell of the drum, sometimes using a stick or a ring on the finger.

Open Tone

The drumhead is struck by the hand at the joints (where the palm and fingers meet), rebounding off the head to let the tone ring out.

Mute Tone

The mute tone is produced by striking the center of the drumhead firmly with the palm of the hand. This produces a tone similar to that of the surdo, but without the articulation of the stick.

chapter four: bass drums

Exercises and Traditional Rhythms

Exercise 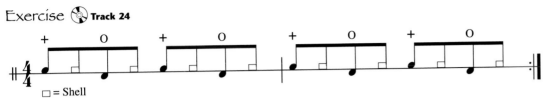 **Track 24**

□ = Shell

Rhythm  **Track 25**

♩ = 80

□ = Shell

8th-note count	1	+	2	+	3	+	4	+	1	+	2	+	3	+	4	+
Tones	+		S	+	O		S	+	+		S	+	O		S	+
Sticking	R		L	R	R		L	R	R		L	R	R		L	R
16th-note count	1	e	+	a	2	e	+	a	3	e	+	a	4	e	+	a

Key

O = Open tone
S = Slap tone
+ = Mute tone
R = Right hand
L = Left hand

chapter five:
single- and multiple-pitched bells

TRIANGLE, COWBELL, AGOGO, GANKOGUI

Within a drumming ensemble, the bell voice, like the bass voice, establishes structural rhythms around which other instruments construct interweaving rhythmic patterns. Depending on the culture, the bell can provide one or more tones. This multiplicity of tones can create a melodic component as well as a rhythmic one. These instruments are made from various metals and alloys and are relatively pitched; they are not tuned to specific pitches and their pitch cannot be easily altered, as can be done for the drums.

Triangle

The *triangle* can be found as far back as the Middle Ages, where it was known as the *sistrum* and featured jingles hung on the bottom leg.[6] The triangle as we know it today is most commonly heard in the orchestra. It produces a high-pitched, sustaining tone, which can serve as a soprano voice within a performing ensemble. Phrasing on the instrument is achieved by combining muffled and sustained tones to create intricate rhythmic patterns. Triangle techniques are as varied as the musical styles in which the instrument is used. In orchestral music, many gauges of metal beaters and triangle sizes are needed, small for a soft sound, and large for a louder sound. In northeastern Brazil, the popular music and dance of *forro* uses a large metal beater and a large triangle to play a constant driving pattern.

Tuning

Triangles are technically classified as *instruments of indefinite pitch*; however, triangles do come in many sizes that vary in pitch. Smaller instruments produce higher pitches and larger instruments produce lower pitches. Sometimes, though, very large homemade triangles are high-pitched, so always choose by tone and not by size.

Playing Position

The triangle can be held in any number of ways. Commonly, a string is tied at one corner of the triangle and held in the weak hand. Wrap the loose end of the string around your index finger and secure its position with the thumb. In contemporary orchestral applications, the string is fastened to a metal or wood clamp that can be hung on a stand for hands-free access. The triangle is hung in the loop of the string, allowing it to vibrate freely. In some traditional settings, a very large triangle is held in the hand without any string at all. When in correct position, the triangle should rest against the palm of the hand. In this position, the performer can execute the strokes and produce the tones necessary for accurate rhythmic phrasing.

Performance Technique

Hold the beater between the index finger and thumb, and curl the fingers loosely around the beater. Strike the triangle with a loose wrist in an even, up-and-downstroke. Playing the inside of the triangle, strike the horizontal leg on the downstroke and the angled leg on the upstroke. Use this technique to execute rolls

[6]Blades, James. "Triangle" The New Grove Dictionary Of Music & Musicians, Macmillan Publishers Ltd., New York, 1980, Volume 19, pp. 137-139

and rhythmic patterns that consist of constant eighth or sixteenth notes. Another technique is to strike the outside of the triangle on the angled leg. This is used when playing medium-tempo syncopated patterns as for the bossa nova. With any style of music, it is important to have a selection of triangles and beaters. Each beater will produce a different sound on the triangle.

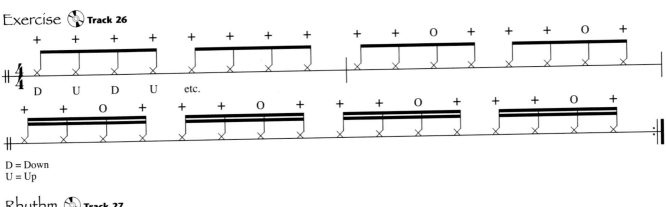

Open Tone

Open tones are produced by removing all fingers from around the triangle, allowing the instrument to vibrate freely. The tone is bright and resonant.

Muffled Tone

Muffle tones are achieved by wrapping the fingers around the triangle, stopping the free vibration. The tone is short, dry and soft.

Written music uses the following symbols to indicate the type of tone to be produced: O=Open tone, +=Muffle tone

Exercises and Traditional Rhythms

Exercise 🔘 **Track 26**

D = Down
U = Up

Rhythm 🔘 **Track 27**

♩ = 96

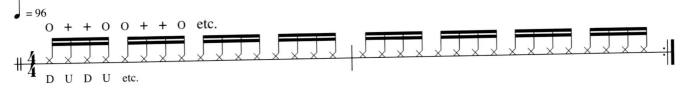

8th-note count	1	+	2	+	3	+	4	+	1	+	2	+	3	+	4	+
Tones	O	+	+	O	O	+	+	O	O	+	+	O	O	+	+	O
Sticking	D	U	D	U	D	U	D	U	D	U	D	U	D	U	D	U
16th-note count	1	e	+	a	2	e	+	a	3	e	+	a	4	e	+	a

Key
O = Open tone
+ = Mute tone
D = Down
U = Up

Cowbell

Cowbells are instruments that originated as their name suggests, as bells suspended from the necks of herded animals.[7] The familiar modern instrument has evolved to a bell without a clapper, requiring the performer to use a stick or mallet to produce sound. The cowbell is capable of varying tones that can be used effectively in phrasing traditional rhythmic patterns. In Cuban music, the cowbells are played by a timbale player who would have two or more mounted on the drums, and a bongo player who would play holding the bell.

[7]Blades, James. Percussion Instruments and Their History, Faber and Faber Ltd., London, 1974

Tuning

Cowbells are instruments of indefinite pitch, with the exception of the *almglocken*, which are tuned chromatically and can span the range of over four octaves. Cowbells come in a variety of sizes and therefore a variety of pitches. In Cuban music, the characteristic of a given musical style is an important factor in choosing a cowbell. The most commonly used are the four- or five-inch bell for cha-cha, and the six- to nine-inch bell for mambo.

Playing Position

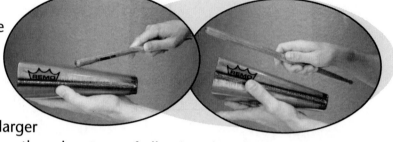

The cowbell should be held in the palm of the weak hand with the mouth facing away from the body. In an ensemble, a solo bell player holds the bell in one hand and strikes it with a 5/16-inch or larger stick. Mounting bells on a stand has the advantage of allowing the player to execute multiple rhythmic parts. This setup is usually used by the timbale player.

Performance Technique

There are two main areas of a cowbell played in any style: the *mouth*, or open end, and the *body*, which is the surface between the mouth and the back of the bell. The mouth of the bell gives the fullest tone and the body produces a higher-pitch tone. With a stick held in the dominant hand using a natural relaxed grip, the cowbell may be struck in the middle of its body or at the mouth. Each area produces a different tone. The combination of tones shape and define the musical phrases. The hand holding the bell can control the length of the sustain by applying and removing finger contact on the bell, producing closed and open tones, respectively.

Open/Closed Tones

The tones of the hand-held cowbells are controlled by the fingers. Open tones are produced by lifting the fingers off the bell while striking its mouth or body. Gripping the bell with the fingers produces closed tones.

Written music uses the following symbols to indicate the type of tone to be produced:

O=Open mouth of bell, B=Body or middle part of bell, += Closed, o=Open

Exercises and Traditional Rhythms

Rhythm Track 28

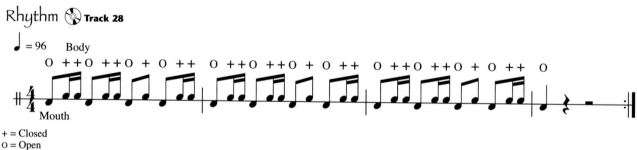

+ = Closed
o = Open

8th-note count	1	+	2	+	3	+	4	+	1	+	2	+	3	+	4	+
Rhythm	M		B	B	M		B	B	M		B		M		B	B
Tones	O		+	+	O		+	+	O		+		O		+	+
16th-note count	1	e	+	a	2	e	+	a	3	e	+	a	4	e	+	a

Key
M = Mouth of bell
B = Body of bell
O = Open tone
+ = Mute tone

Agogo

The *agogo* (AH-goh-goh) is a set of single, double or triple bells on one handle. Its origins are believed to be among the Yorob, Igala, and Edo speaking people of Nigeria.[8] Like most bells, its function is to mark structural beats within complex rhythmic patterns. The agogo is most recognized for its role in the Brazilian samba as well as in Afro-Brazilian religious ceremonies. It is also used in popular secular music like maracatu, baion and other traditional music of Brazil.

Tuning

The agogo bells are classified as instruments of indefinite pitch; however, the interval of a perfect fifth is common among the relative pitches of the bells.

Playing Position

Hold the agogo in the weak hand with the thumb on top of the small bell and the fingers around the rod that connects the two bells. Use a thick drumstick and strike the side of the bells.

Performance Technique

The bells are played on the side of the instrument's body. The low tones generally mark the downbeats and the high tones complete the rhythmic patterns. More complex rhythmic figures can be achieved by squeezing the handle of the bells so that the bells contact each other. This technique produces a subtle click that can be used to fill in around structural rhythms, creating a steady pulse of notes common to the rhythm instruments (see "Chapter Six: Rhythm Instruments").

The following symbols are used to indicate the desired tones.

H=High, L=Low

Exercises and Traditional Rhythms

Rhythm 🔊 **Track 29**

♩ = 105

8th-note count	1	+	2	+	3	+	4	+	1	+	2	+	3	+	4	+
Rhythm	L				H	H	L	L	L		H	H	L			L
Sticking	R				R	R	R	R	R		R	R	R			R
16th-note count	1	e	+	a	2	e	+	a	3	e	+	a	4	e	+	a

Key

H = High tone
L = Low tone

[8]Gourlay, K.A. and Schechter, John M. "Agogo" <u>The New Grove Dictionary of Musical Instruments</u>, Macmillan Publishers Ltd., New York, 1984, Volume 1, pp. 32-33

Gankogui

The *gankogui* (gahn-KOE-gwee, also spelled *gongoque*) is a double bell similar to the *agogo*. It is common to the music of Ghana and Togo. The bells have no internal clappers and must be played with a stick. The gankogui functions much as other bells do in that it marks structural beats of complex rhythms used in dance and ceremony. Although there are two bells on the gankogui, it is common to use only the high bell; however, the low bell can be used to mark downbeats or other significant beats within the rhythmic cycle or repeated rhythmic pattern.

Playing Position

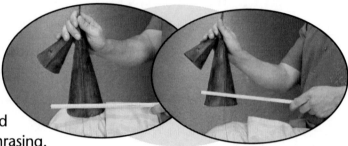

The bells are played with the dominant hand and held out in front of the body with the small bell on top and the opening facing away from the performer. Playing with the dominant hand allows the performer to play with the control and dexterity required for quick rhythms or subtle phrasing.

Performance Technique

The grip on the stick should be loose and relaxed. The natural curve of the fingers should cradle the stick in the hand. As soon as a sensation of tension is felt in the hands or fingers, stop and relax the fingers to regain the original relaxed, natural grip. Tension in the hands and fingers create a hard stroke, which does not allow the stick and hand to move efficiently or to effectively absorb the shock of impact. These results will negatively affect instrument tone, cause injury to the performer's wrists, and cause the instrument to break.

The types of strokes that are used for the gankogui are the same for each bell. The stroke should move in a straight line to and from the bell with the palm of the hand facing down. Dynamics are achieved by increasing or decreasing the distance the stick travels to the bell. A *piano* or soft dynamic might require a three-inch stroke, and a *forte* or loud dynamic might require a nine-inch stroke.

The types of tones characteristic of the gankogui are the *open tone* and the *closed tone*.

Open Tone

The open tone is produced by allowing the stick to rebound immediately from the bell upon impact. The sound of the tone is full and resonant. This is the most common tone used in performance.

Closed Tone

The sound of this tone is muffled and short. The stroke initially begins like the open stroke; however, instead of allowing the stick to naturally rebound, it is pressed into the bell. The bell can also be muffled by pressing it against the performer's leg.

Exercises and Traditional Rhythms

Rhythm 🎵 **Track 30**

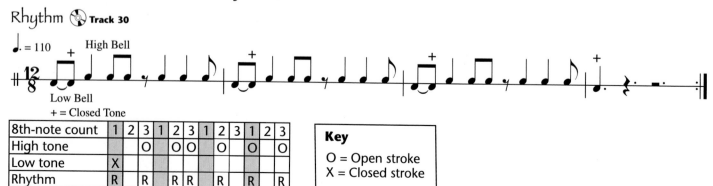

8th-note count	1	2	3	1	2	3	1	2	3	1	2	3
High tone			O		O	O		O		O		O
Low tone	X											
Rhythm	R		R		R	R		R		R		R

Key

O = Open stroke
X = Closed stroke

chapter six:
rhythm instruments

SHEKERE, GANZA, CABASA, SNARE DRUM, MARACAS, GUIRO

All cultures utilize rhythm instruments such as drums, cymbals, shakers, rattles and scrapers of some variety. The names and construction of these instruments differ from culture to culture; however, their function remains the same. These rhythm instruments of indefinite pitch usually provide a steady rhythmic pattern over which other specialized patterns are articulated. They are essential to establishing the feel of the musical style. A common misconception of rhythm instruments is that they can be shaken or scraped at random. The performer shortly realizes the power of the instrument and that the patterns must fit the music and eventually define the rhythm. Because these instruments are so fundamental in design and appear in music all around the world, it is difficult to follow an extended history of their evolution.

Shekere

The *shekere* (SHAY-ker-ray) is an example of a rattle with external beads. (The small version is also called the *axatse* [a-HAH-chee].) Typically, the shekere consists of a dried gourd and is fitted with a net of beads that is wrapped around the bulb of the gourd. The gourd can be whole or cut at the small end with the inside cleaned of all seeds and loose material. The size of the instrument can vary from a small, hand-held instrument to one that requires both hands for accurate control of the rhythm. This instrument is common to much of the music of Africa.

Playing Position

The instrument is cradled in the hands with the large part of the gourd resting in the dominant hand. The gourd should be held away from the body so that it is free to move in the hands of the performer.

axatse

Performance Technique

Once the shekere is in its playing position, the rhythmic possibilities are vast. The beads around the gourd are capable of producing sound as the instrument is activated. The beads rebound after the initial activation. There are several different strokes used in shekere performance. The stroke types are downstroke, upstroke, outstroke and bass tone. The hands should move in parallel motion maintaining the same distance between them as they perform the designated stroke types.

Downstroke

This stroke is achieved by dropping the hands nine to twelve inches, followed by a quick rebound in the opposite direction. This quick change of direction forces the instrument down into the dominant hand, producing the sound of the beads slapping against the outside of the gourd.

Upstroke

This stroke is actually a follow-through to the downstroke. Immediately after the completion of the downstroke, the shekere returns to the starting position. As with the downstroke, an abrupt stopping of the motion will cause the beads to slap against the gourd, producing the sound.

Outstroke

This stroke is achieved by pushing the top of the shekere out and away from the body after an upstroke. The momentum of the upstroke aids in producing the outstroke. This stroke enables the performance of fast, rhythmic figures.

Bass tone

The bass tone is produced by striking the bottom, unbeaded portion of the instrument, producing a low, resonant tone. Although there is sympathetic activation of the beads, the low bass tone is the primary sound produced.

The combination of these strokes creates intricate rhythms and phrasings. Once the individual sounds are produced consistently, the combination of the techniques can produce residual sounds such as a back slap from the beads. Back slap is the sound made from the beads hitting the gourd, caused by rebound from the execution of the various stroke types.

Exercises and Traditional Rhythms

Rhythm Track 31

♩ = 105

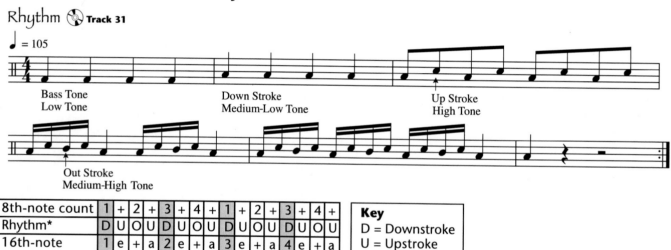

Bass Tone
Low Tone

Down Stroke
Medium-Low Tone

Up Stroke
High Tone

Out Stroke
Medium-High Tone

8th-note count	1	+	2	+	3	+	4	+	1	+	2	+	3	+	4	+
Rhythm*	D	U	O	U	D	U	O	U	D	U	O	U	D	U	O	U
16th-note count	1	e	+	a	2	e	+	a	3	e	+	a	4	e	+	a

Key
D = Downstroke
U = Upstroke
O = Outstroke

* This pattern may be changed to any repetitive rhythm.

Ganza

The *ganza* (gahn-ZAH) type of shaker is constructed of a metal tube, partially filled with small beads or metal balls and capped on both ends. Generally, the tubes are pre-filled, but some modern manufacturers allow the addition or subtraction of beads. The ganza (which can be referred to as *chocalho*) accompanies traditional dance and popular music of Brazil. The correct phrasing of the ganza pattern establishes authenticity of the samba style. Like all types of shakers, the ganza anchors all syncopated rhythms with a constant sixteenth-note feel. The addition of accents creates unique rhythmic styles found in many cultures.

Playing Position

Depending on the size of the instrument, hold the ganza with one or two hands, approximately at chest level.

Performance Technique

The ganza is shaken using the wrists and forearms, using an even, back-and-forth motion. The beads hit the inside of the cylinder, creating a steady rhythmic pulse. Slightly tilt the cylinder to one side so the beads rest at one end. This will help control the beads. A variety of tones can be achieved with a cylinder of this type or any shaped shaker. Try swirling the tube as evenly as possible. Start slowly and increase speed for special effects.

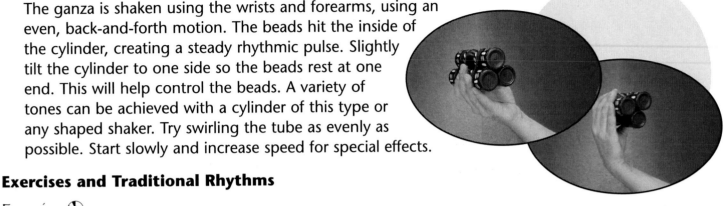

Exercises and Traditional Rhythms

Exercise 🎧 **Track 32**

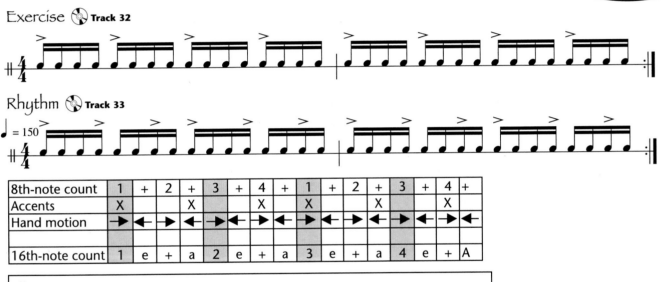

Rhythm 🎧 **Track 33**

♩ = 150

8th-note count	1	+	2	+	3	+	4	+	1	+	2	+	3	+	4	+
Accents	X			X			X		X			X			X	
Hand motion	→	←	→	←	→	←	→	←	→	←	→	←	→	←	→	←
16th-note count	1	e	+	a	2	e	+	a	3	e	+	a	4	e	+	A

Key

X = Accent rhythm

← → = Forward and backward motions

Tip: Start with the shaker in the preparatory motion backward to get beads in position for the downbeat.

Cabasa

The *cabasa* (ka-BAH-sah, also called *cabaça*, *afochê* or *afoxê*) combines scraping and rattle principles. This instrument originated in the Latin American dance band as a gourd wrapped with beads, similar to the shekere; however, the gourd was turned to allow the beads to scrape along the outside. The construction of the modern instrument connects a handle to a cylinder covered with a textured piece of sheet metal, that is then loosely wrapped with ball chain.

Tuning

The cabasa is an instrument of indefinite pitch, and therefore has no tuning capabilities.

Playing Position

The cabasa is held by the handle in the dominant hand, with the head of the instrument resting in the palm of the weak hand. The fingers of the weak hand should curve around the beads on the head of the instrument.

Performance Technique

The cabasa can be played using two primary techniques: *turning* and *shaking*. The turning stroke is achieved by maintaining contact between the beads and the hand. Holding the beads in place while turning the handle of the cabasa produces the desired rhythm. The desired length of the sound is obtained by varying the duration of strokes. Rhythmic patterns use sequences of forward and backward turns. Phrasing and musical nuance are achieved by the directional sequence of the turning strokes. A *forward turn* is defined as a motion that rotates the cabasa away from the body. A *reverse turn* is defined as a motion that rotates the cabasa toward the body.

The second technique used for cabasa performance is a technique used on the maracas. By either shaking or striking the head of the instrument onto the palm of the cupped hand, a short sound is produced that is ideal for delicate rhythmic patterns.

Exercises and Traditional Rhythms

Rhythm (🎵) **Track 34**

♩ = 96

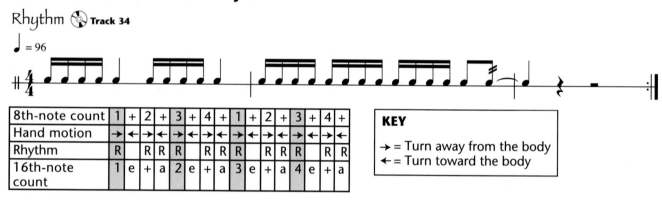

8th-note count	1	+	2	+	3	+	4	+	1	+	2	+	3	+	4	+
Hand motion	→	←	→	←	→	←	→	←	→	←	→	←	→	←	→	←
Rhythm	R		R	R	R		R	R	R		R	R	R		R	R
16th-note count	1	e	+	a	2	e	+	a	3	e	+	a	4	e	+	a

KEY

→ = Turn away from the body
← = Turn toward the body

Snare Drum

The *snare drum*, adapted to the modern drumset, evolved from military use similar to the bass drum. The snare drum is a double-headed instrument with the unique feature of 8 to 20 strands of wire, or cables called *snares*, stretched in rows across the bottom head. It is generally medium-high (mezzo-soprano) to high (soprano) in pitch, and can dynamically cut over the ensemble and function as a call instrument.[9] It can be utilized as a rhythm instrument to hold down a repeated pattern, or emphasize key points in a rhythm by accenting them. Within the drumset, the snare provides punctuation to accent and rhythm; within the drum ensemble, it provides excellent support to the rhythmic style. In countries that celebrated the Catholic pre-Lenten festivities called Carnaval, the snare would be incorporated into the annual parade. This type of parading and playing can be quite challenging.

Tuning

The snare drum can be tuned using a cross or circular tuning system. In either case, each tension point must be of equal pitch, and a moderately high pitch should be achieved. Care should be taken to not let the pitch get too high, as this will eliminate the characteristic resonance of the instrument and make it sound more like a contemporary marching snare drum.

[9]Blades, James. Percussion Instruments and Their History, Faber and Faber Ltd., London, 1974

Playing Position

When stationary, the snare drum is placed on a stand. In countries like Brazil and Cuba, the performer uses a strap in a variety of ways.

1. Wear the strap around the neck and shoulder, much like the surdo. Suspend the drum on the weak side of the body at waist level, with the playing surface angled toward the strong side of the body. The drum can rest on the upper leg.

2. Wear the strap around the waist and attach the hook on a tuning lug.

Performance Technique

The standard matched grip works well when the snare is held on a stand. Traditional grip can be used when using a strap. This technique is common in countries with pre-Lenten Carnaval celebrations, where walking and playing becomes a challenge. The strokes as well as the drum positioning must be precise. When wearing a strap, the drum can move slightly and change position, making it difficult to get a consistent rim shot. With your stick held in the matched or traditional grip, practice walking and playing until you control the drum's movement with each step.

Open Tones

Open tones are generally performed by playing the drum slightly off-center. This area produces the most resonant tone; the center of the drum produces a very dry tone. Experiment with tonal variations by playing on different areas of the drumhead; notice how this can enhance the phrasing and musical subtleties of rhythms.

Rim Shots

Rim shots are performed by striking the rim and drumhead simultaneously. This technique produces a very sharp and projecting tone. Rim shots can be used to mark significant beats or to bring out phrases within more complex rhythmic patterns.

Rim Tones

Rim tones are played on the rim only. This technique produces short, clicking tones. This can be used to vary or substitute for open tones.

Exercises and Traditional Rhythms

Rhythm Track 35

8th-note count	1	+	2	+	3	+	4	+	1	+	2	+	3	+	4	+
Rhythm	rs	x	x	rs	x	x	rs	x	x	Bz	x	x	x	Bz	x	x
Sticking	R	L	R	L	R	L	R	L	R	L	R	L	R	L	R	L
16th-note count	1	e	+	a	2	e	+	a	3	e	+	a	4	e	+	a

Key
x = Softer
rs = Rim shot
Bz = Buzz tone
R = Right hand
L = Left hand

Maracas

Examples of *maracas* and similar instruments can be found around the world as various varieties of rattles. The familiar maraca, a round gourd fastened to a handle, originates from Venezuela.[10] These instruments can provide steady rhythmic support within an ensemble as well as perform extremely complex polyrhythms as solo instruments. The maracas often fill the gaps in syncopated rhythms.

Tuning

Maracas are relative-pitched instruments and are not tunable. Their timbre depends on the material used to make them. Generally, synthetic materials are brighter and louder than natural materials.

Playing Position

The maracas are held by the handles, with the index finger extended onto the bulb. This provides the performer with more control of the instruments.

Performance Technique

Hold one maraca in each hand. Grasp the handle of each using a matched grip position as you would a drumstick, with your thumb, index finger and three smallest fingers around the handle. Using your wrist, make a sharp, downward, snapping stroke. The beads inside the maraca will hit against the inner wall, creating a "chik" sound. To create the most preferable sound, it is important that the beads strike against the inner wall all together. Extending the index fingers toward the shell will give you more control of how the beads fall inside the shell.

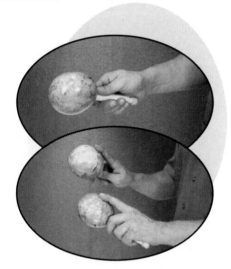

Exercises and Traditional Rhythms

Rhythm (no track)

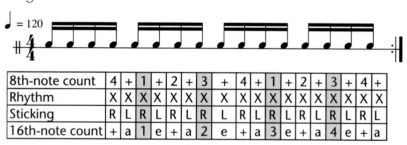

♩ = 120

8th-note count	4	+	1	+	2	+	3	+	4	+	1	+	2	+	3	+	4	+
Rhythm	X	X	X	X	X	X	X	X	X	X	X	X	X	X	X	X	X	X
Sticking	R	L	R	L	R	L	R	L	R	L	R	L	R	L	R	L	R	L
16th-note count	+	a	1	e	+	a	2	e	+	a	3	e	+	a	4	e	+	a

Guiro

The *guiro* (GWEE-roe) is an example of a scraper made from a dried gourd that is common to music of Latin America, the Caribbean, Panama and South America. The gourd must be long and narrow in shape, with slits made across its width. By scraping a small stick across the ridges, the performer creates rhythms, and by controlling the length and articulation of each stroke, produces style-defining phrasing. Modern plastic instruments have been developed and can be used as effectively as natural instruments.

[10]Leake, Jerry. Series A.I.M. Percussion Text: Volume I, Afro-American Aspects, Rhombus Publishing, Boston, 1993

Tuning

The guiro is an instrument of indefinite pitch, and therefore cannot be tuned to play specific pitches.

Playing Position

The guiro is held in the weak hand and slightly to the performer's weak side, with the opening facing out. The holding hand should be out and away from the body in order to facilitate any movements necessary for phrasing and rhythmic subtleties. The guiro is played with a small, thin scraper held in the dominant hand.

Performance Technique

The challenge of playing the guiro with musical accuracy is understanding the subtle changes necessary during performance. The basic stroke uses a back-and-forth motion across the length of the notched area. Phrasing and rhythmic variation are achieved by breaking and continuing contact with the instrument while maintaining a steady pulse. The following sequence will develop the basic guiro pattern when played together.

Downstroke

The guiro is played with one stroke, beginning on the part of the instrument closest to the body and moving away. This stroke should use the entire notched area and maintain the same velocity throughout its duration.

Upstroke

The upstroke simply returns to the starting position, with the same attention to speed and contact as for the downstroke.

Full Stroke

With the guiro in the playing position, use one unbroken motion to scrape away from the body and then immediately reverse direction back towards the body. The full stroke should maintain the same speed throughout its duration, and should use the entire notched area. Once an even and smooth stroke has been attained, play them in repetition, separating each with a small break in contact.

The basic guiro pattern is as follows: full stroke, downstroke, upstroke. Repeat this sequence in time; the full stroke takes one beat, and the downstroke and upstroke each take one-half beat. When the sequence is performed correctly, the playing hand should visually appear to be moving up and down on the surface of the guiro in an even, repetitive motion.

Exercises and Traditional Rhythms

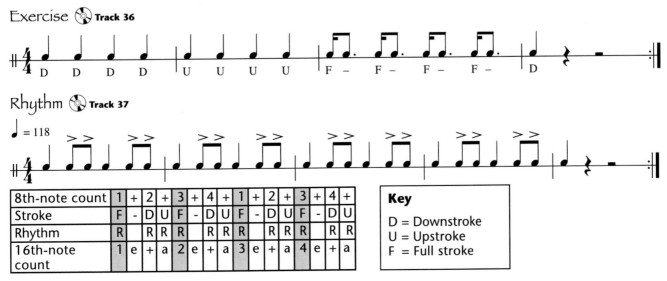

8th-note count	1	+	2	+	3	+	4	+	1	+	2	+	3	+	4	+
Stroke	F	-	D	U	F	-	D	U	F	-	D	U	F	-	D	U
Rhythm	R		R	R	R		R	R	R		R	R	R		R	R
16th-note count	1	e	+	a	2	e	+	a	3	e	+	a	4	e	+	a

Key

D = Downstroke
U = Upstroke
F = Full stroke

chapter seven:
instruments of variable pitch

TALKING DRUM, CUICA, BERIMBAU

Instruments of variable pitch, like other instruments in this book, appear in many different cultures around the world. They serve functions of communication, replicate the human voice and provide melodic texture. In traditional settings, these instruments have very specific and complex histories. It is not the intent of this book to delve into details of these deep traditions, but to introduce the basic elements that make each unique.

Talking Drum

With its roots in Nigeria, the *talking drum* is a most interesting instrument. Its variable pitch allows the performer intricate control over phrasing. This drum is shaped like an hourglass, with a drumhead on both ends linked by a rope or long cord. Depending on the size and tension put on the heads, this instrument can span many voice ranges in the performing ensemble, from high (soprano) to medium-low (tenor).

Tuning

The fundamental tuning of the talking drum should be at a pitch that is as low as possible without losing tone and resonance. This pitch level varies among instruments and head types. Generally speaking, a medium tuning works adequately. This enables maximum pitch range.

Playing Position

The traditional instrument placement is under the weak arm of the performer with a strap placed over the shoulder. The fingers of the weak hand grip the ropes or gut that connects both heads. The stick is held in the dominant hand.

Performance Technique

The drum is played on the front head. Pitch variation is achieved by squeezing the ropes with the weak hand. Additional pressure can be applied to the ropes by pressing the elbow of the weak arm against the drum, forcing it against the performer's ribs. It is important to become familiar with the points that produce specific pitches. Producing pitches accurately and consistently is essential to constructing melodic phrases.

Exercises and Traditional Rhythms

Exercise 🎧 Track 38

Rhythm 🎧 Track 39

♩. = 100

8th-note count	1	2	3	4	5	6	1	2	3	4	5	6
Rhythm	X		X		X	X		X		X		X
High tone			O		O	O		O		O		O
Low tone	O											
Sticking	R		R		R	R		R		R		R
16th-note count	1	e	a	2	e	a	3	e	a	4	e	a

Cuíca

The *cuica* (koo-EE-kah), also called *kwita* [Zaire], *puita*, *boi* and *onca* [Latin America][11]) is similar to the talking drum in that its pitch can be altered to create interesting rhythmic patterns. Believed to have been introduced to Brazil by Bantu slaves, the cuica has been known in Spain for centuries, and Muslims introduced it to Africa. It is a single-headed cylinder with a rattan or bamboo dowel inserted throughout the head's center. The sound is produced when a damp cloth is pulled along the dowel. The cuica is a rhythm instrument as well as a solo instrument. Staying on a rhythm pattern can create a theme in a percussion arrangement. A master cuica player would use the sounds of the drum to "sing" melodies. The voice of this instrument within the performing ensemble ranges from medium-high (alto) to high (soprano).

Tuning

In the *Carioca* style, the cuica is tuned to a very high pitch. This allows it to project when played outdoors with large percussion ensembles, as is common. A lower-tuned cuica recreates the sound of the cuicas before tuning mechanisms were developed.

Playing Position

The performer can play the cuica sitting down or standing in either of two positions. The Carioca player would use a strap around the neck or shoulder with the open end of the drum against the midsection, using the middle and ring finger of the weak hand to press against the drumhead to change the pitch. The dominant hand reaches inside the drum to gain access to the dowel. The cuica can also be played with the shell of the drum held horizontally, pressing the drumhead with the thumb to change the pitch.

Performance Technique

The dominant hand gently slides a damp rag along the bamboo stick with a back-and-forth motion as the weak hand presses against the center of the drumhead, causing the pitch to change. The goal is to produce a consistent tone throughout the up-and-down stroke. The action is smooth, and if a louder and more curious sound is desired, slight pressure can be added to the rag using the thumb and index finger. A common misconception is that the stick is pulled to produce the tones; this is not correct, as pulling on the dowel will cause it to break.

Open Tone

The open tone is produced with the fingers off the drumhead, holding the cloth between the thumb and the index finger and squeezing it lightly against the stick while sliding it up and down to produce the sound. Most of the strokes are played on the stick within the first three inches from the drumhead. This helps prevent the stick from breaking. Only play the entire length of the stick for long notes.

Closed Tone

With the finger on the drumhead, the pitch may be varied by pressing and releasing the head while sliding the cloth up and down the stick.

[11]Schechter, John M. "Cuica" The New Grove Dictionary of Musical Instruments, Macmillan Publishers Ltd., New York, 1984, Volume 1, pp. 527

Press Tone

The key to a great sound on the cuica is the correct combination of pressure on the drumhead and on the cloth squeezing the stick. The basic tones are high and low, produced by pressing and releasing the cloth as it slides up and down the stick. Experiment by applying various degrees of pressure, listening to the tone created each time. Remember that small incremental movements are all that are needed.

The following symbols are used to indicate the desired tones.

O=Open, +=Closed

Exercises and Traditional Rhythms

Exercise 🎵 **Track 40**

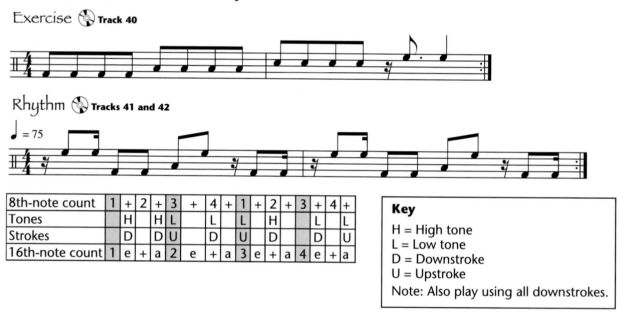

Rhythm 🎵 **Tracks 41 and 42**

♩ = 75

8th-note count	1	+	2	+	3	+	4	+	1	+	2	+	3	+	4	+
Tones	H		H	L		L		L	H			L			L	
Strokes	D		D	U		D		U	D			D			D	U
16th-note count	1	e	+	a	2	e	+	a	3	e	+	a	4	e	+	a

Key

H = High tone
L = Low tone
D = Downstroke
U = Upstroke
Note: Also play using all downstrokes.

Berimbau

The *berimbau* (BARE-eem-bow) is a Brazilian musical bow of Angola origin, and is also called the *oricongo* or *aricungo*. It adds a unique color to any type of percussion ensemble when featured. Traditionally, it is made from a branch of the biriba tree. Instruments that are more modern are made from other materials like bamboo. The berimbau is bent in an arc, with a wire string attached to both ends and an open gourd attached to the bow that acts as a resonator. With the bow held against the player's abdomen, the metal string is struck with a thin stick held in the player's hand along with a basket shaker called the *caxixi* (ka-SHEE-shee). The timbre is altered as the performer moves the resonator toward and away from the abdomen. Placing a coin or stone against the metal string changes the pitch. The primary function of this instrument is to provide dance accompaniment for the Bahian *capoiera* (Brazilian Martial Arts).[12] Traditionally, the ensemble plays in a circle, or *roda*, with pandeiros, hand claps and agogo. Songs related to the fight of the capoeira, referred to as the "game," are sung over the instrument's accompaniment. The ensemble must be dynamically sensitive to allow the berimbau to be heard.

[12]Schecter, John M.. "Berimbau" The New Grove Dictionary Of Music & Musicians Macmillan Publishers Ltd., New York, 1980, Volume 2, pp. 553-554

Tuning

The gourd is the berimbau's resonator and the open end is called the mouth. The gourd is prepared with a loop of string at the bottom. Once the bow is pulled tight with the cord secured at the top, slip the loop around the lower end of the instrument so both the bow and wire go through it. Moving the gourd up and down the bow raises and lowers the pitch, respectively. The larger the gourd, the louder the sound, but this is not always desired. Your goal is to match the bow and gourd to obtain a wah-wah effect, and using a small gourd generally gets this sound.

Playing Position

The berimbau is not easy to hold without a little discomfort, especially when first attempting to play, and it may take a few minutes to adjust. Hold the bow with the dominant hand. With the gourd already in place, position the little finger under the string. The mouth of the gourd should be in the center of your abdomen. The hand holding the bow holds the stone or coin between the thumb and index finger while the middle and ring fingers wrap around the bow. Move the coin or stone back and forth to the metal string. As you begin to play, keep the bow perpendicular to the ground and be sure not to twist the position of the gourd.

Performance Technique

Hold the caxixi and stick in the dominant hand. The caxixi is heard when playing the bass, treble and buzz tones and is also played independently. Use a sharp downward motion to create the best sound as beads strike the bottom of the caxixi.

There are three basic tones produced on the berimbau: bass tone, treble tone and buzz tone.

Bass Tone

Without contacting the wire string with the coin/stone, strike the metal string just below the coin position to produce the bass open tone.

Treble Tone

Move the coin against the string to change pitch while striking it above the coin position.

Buzz Tone

Touch the coin lightly to the metal string and strike the string above the coin position.

The position of the gourd may effect the quality of these tones. These include an open gourd and closed gourd.

Gourd Open (Away from Body)

Turning the gourd out and away from the body allows the tone to resonate.

Gourd Closed (Against Body)

Turning the gourd in toward the body muffles the tone.

A quick open-and-close motion with the gourd creates a wah-wah effect used in many rhythms of the berimbau.

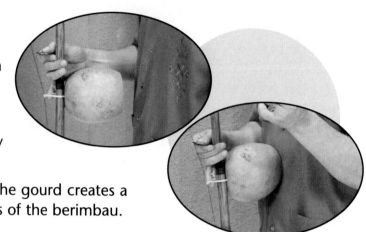

Exercises and Traditional Rhythms

Exercise 🔘 **Track 43**

Rhythm 🔘 **Track 44**

Key

+ = Mute tone
o = Open tone
≥ = Wah-wah
▲ = Caxixi
× = Coin
● = Raise pitch

chapter eight:
call drums

TIMBALE, REPINIQUE

The drums in this chapter represent those that function as the ensemble leader. Call and response is a principle element of form in compositions for drumming ensemble. Many cultures designate one player or instrument to the leader, who, through specific rhythms, communicates to the ensemble members what to do next. These drums are either very large in size, like the *atsimevu* of the Ewe drummers in Ghana, or they are very high in pitch like the *repique* of Brazil. Regardless of the physical characteristics of the drum, the function remains the same—to attract the attention of the players and communicate performance cues.

Timbale

The *timbale* (tim-BAH-lay) is often found in the dance music of Latin America. Commonly referred to in the plural, *timbales* refers to a set of two or four drums, 13 and 14 inches in diameter, that fall in the medium-high (mezzo-soprano) to high (soprano) voice range. The shells are usually made of metal, but wood shells can also be found. Cowbells are frequently seen mounted between the drums. The timbale drums function as the timekeeper as well as the leader by signaling the opening and closing of a musical arrangement with the *abanico* beat (a beat consisting of a series of rim shots and rolls). The word abanico means "fan," and is a "call" used in Latin salsa music. The rim shot and *cascara* (playing on the shell) techniques produce very loud, cutting tones that can be heard over the loudest ensembles. The timbale drums have been embraced by many musical styles all over the world. They appeared in Cuba in the 1940s and found a place in traditional *charanga* music, and their use became common in R & B, Latin-rock and disco music when they came into popularity in the 1970s. Timbales quickly became the instrument of choice to be featured with solos that enhance the musical feel and style.

Tuning
A standard size for the small drum is 13 inches, and 14 inches is standard for the large drum. The pitches are tuned high to low, generally a fourth apart. Tune the high drum to approximately C5.

Playing Position
Timbales are played with two drumsticks held in a matched grip position. Right-handed players set the drums up with the smallest on the right. Left-hand players should reverse this arrangement.

Performance Technique
The timbales are a driving force when they appear in any ensemble, providing a steady, syncopated rhythmic pattern. This pattern is played on the cowbells with the dominant hand, while the other strikes the drumhead with a combination of open and muted tones. This combination of tones is called the *tumbao*, or basic beat.

Cascara (Paila)

Playing the sides of the shell is called cascara or paila, and is used when playing a folk style of rumba. Typically, a cowbell would be mounted in the center between the two drums or horizontally over the small drum.

Open Tone

Strike the drumhead in the center with a drumstick, and let the stick rebound off the playing surface, allowing the sound to ring out.

Closed Tone

This stroke is performed exactly like the open tone with one exception: Prevent the natural rebound by applying pressure to the tip of the stick upon impact. This will impair the sustain of the drumhead, producing a short, dry tone.

Rim Shot

The rim shot is achieved by striking the rim and the drumhead simultaneously.

Finger Stroke

Hold the stick in the weak hand between the index finger and thumb. It should rest in the first knuckle of the index finger. Strike the drum with the fingers, making sure the stick does not contact the drum, and play cascara with the dominant hand.

Exercises and Traditional Rhythms

Abanico Call-In 🔘 Track 45

Abanico Call-in

× = Rimshot

Rhythm 1 🔘 Track 46

♩ = 110
Timbale = R.H.

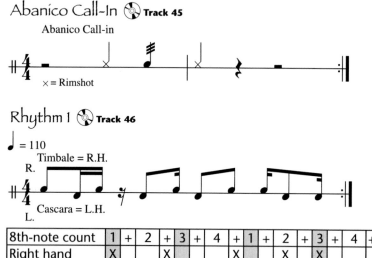

Cascara = L.H.

8th-note count	1	+	2	+	3	+	4	+	1	+	2	+	3	+	4	+
Right hand	X				X				X				X		X	
Left hand			X				X				X				X		X
16th-note count	1	e	+	a	2	e	+	a	3	e	+	a	4	e	+	a

Key
X = Side of shell
R = Right hand
L = Left hand

Rhythm 2 🔘 Track 47

Cowbell = R.H.
♩ = 110

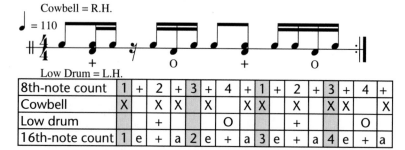

Low Drum = L.H.

8th-note count	1	+	2	+	3	+	4	+	1	+	2	+	3	+	4	+
Cowbell	X		X	X		X		X	X	X		X	X	X		X
Low drum			+				O				+				O	
16th-note count	1	e	+	a	2	e	+	a	3	e	+	a	4	e	+	a

Key
X = Side of shell
O = Open tone
+ = Mute tone
R = Right hand
L = Left hand

Repinique

The *repinique* (he-pen-EEK-ee) is a cylindrical, double-headed drum played by the leader of the Brazilian bateria (percussion ensemble). Introduced in the 1950s, it is a newcomer to the bateria. Considered a tenor drum, it is used to conduct the percussion ensemble through calls signaling the beginnings and endings of rhythmic phrases, and call and response breaks. A conductor cues cadences with hand signals, whistles or both. The rhythmic function of the repinique is to play a steady repetitive pattern that reinforces the more syncopated pattern of the tamborins, agogos and cuicas.

Tuning

Although the repinique is considered a tenor drum in the bateria ensemble, at times it is tuned very high in pitch for specific musical styles. This is done so that it is capable of being heard over very large percussion ensembles. Traditionally, however, its tuning is left to the discretion of the musical director and not tuned to a specific pitch. In the samba-style bateria, the repinique is pitched below the tamborim and above the snare drum. A cross tuning or circular tuning system can be used to equalize each tension point.

Playing Position

In the Carioca style, the repinique is suspended by a strap over the shoulder of the performer. The drum should hang on the performer's weak side with the playing surface facing the dominant side. It is important to keep the drum at a consistent height and angle so the stick strikes in the same spot every time. In a second style of playing from Salvador, Bahia in Brazil, the performer uses two long drumsticks and straps the drum around the waist so that it sits low between the legs. Many drummers mount the repiniques on snare stands in sets of two or three drums, enabling them to play the surdo and repinique rhythms together.

Performance Technique

The repinique is played using the weak hand and a stick held in the dominant hand. In the Carioca style, three basic tones are produced when playing the repinique: the *open tone*, *rim shot*, and *slap tone*.

Open Tone

Using a drumstick, strike the drumhead just off-center with an even stroke, letting the stick rebound and the tone ring out.

Rim Shot

In the same hand position as for the open tone, bring the stick down from center to where the stick is angled touching the drumhead and rim. You must maintain this position consistently to achieve a good rim shot.

Slap Tone

This is done with the bare hand and is similar to the large body drum slaps. Place the hand on the drum rim just above the joint where the fingers and palm meet. You don't

want to hit directly on the joint bones. Keep the thumb away from the rim. Use a smooth, even stroke with a snap to hit the drum. As you strike, keep the hand down slightly, grabbing at the drumhead with the fingertips. This is the same slap technique as used on the large hand drums (see "Chapter One").

Bahian Style

The Bahian style uses two long, thin sticks to produce a series of alternating open and rim shot strokes.

Exercises and Traditional Rhythms

Exercise 1 🎧 **Track 48**

Call-in, Call-out

8th-note count	1	+	2	+	3	+	4	+	1	+	2	+	3	+	4	+
Tones	rs		rs		rs				o	o	o		o	o		o
Sticking	R		R		R				R	R	R		R	R		R
16th-note count	1	e	+	a	2	e	+	a	3	e	+	a	4	e	+	a

Exercise 2 🎧 **Track 49**

Call-in, Call-out

8th-note count	1	+	2	+	3	+	4	+	1	+	2	+	3	+	4	+
Tones	rs	rs		O		O		O		rs	rs	rs	rs		O	
Sticking	R	R		R		R		R		R	R	R	R		R	
16th-note count	1	e	+	a	2	e	+	a	3	e	+	a	4	e	+	a

Rhythm 🎧 **Track 50**

♩ = 114

R L L R L L R L R L R L L R L L

8th-note count	1	+	2	+	3	+	4	+	1	+	2	+	3	+	4	+
Tones	rs	O	O	rs	O	O	rs	O	O	O	rs	O	O	rs	O	O
Sticking	R	L	L	R	L	L	R	L	R	L	R	L	L	R	L	L
16th-note count	1	e	+	a	2	e	+	a	3	e	+	a	4	e	+	a

Key

O = Open tone
rs = Rimshot
R = Right hand
L = Left hand

Tip: The strong note is on the rimshot beats with the right hand. Rhythm can also be played with alternating strokes R L.

chapter nine:

traditional world drumming ensembles

The music of many cultures features percussion ensembles that contain drums ranging from low bass voices to high soprano voices. This chapter features examples of culturally specific drum ensembles, exploring typical arrangements of traditional Arabic, Brazilian, West African and Cuban music. Each ensemble features rhythms and instruments indigenous to the particular culture, and the arrangements are composed following traditional guidelines.

Middle Eastern

This ensemble contains the riqq, tar and doumbek. The rhythm used here is traditionally a call to dance. The arrangement is structured in four-measure phrases. Each four-measure phrase may be repeated at the discretion of the performers before moving to the next phrase. No repeats are marked for ease in illustrating the overall arrangement. Each phrase can be repeated to extend solos and ensemble sections.

Track 51

Middle Eastern

Frank Kumor

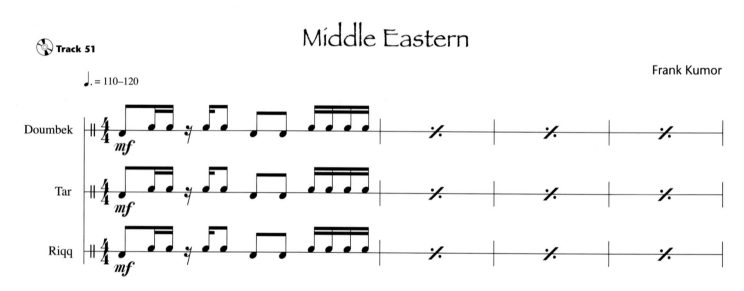

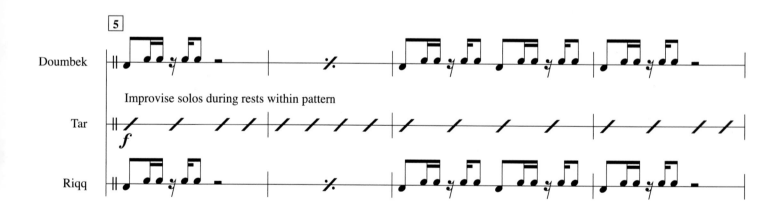

Improvise solos during rests within pattern

West African

This ensemble features a West African dance rhythm in triple meter. The arrangement uses the call and response style common to many cultures. The lead drummer plays the initial rhythm or "call," which is "answered" by the ensemble. Each section is repeated until the lead drummer plays the call, signaling the beginning of the next section. Let each rhythm settle into a comfortable groove before calling the next section. Once you get comfortable, begin to experiment with different sounds. If there is more than one player per part, then each player on the same part must play the same sequence of tones. The most important thing to remember is to be sure that you are using correct technique at all times. Don't cheat your tones.

African

Frank Kumor

Cuban Rumba Guaguanco

One of the most popular styles of rumba is called the *guaguanco* from Havana, Cuba. It can be heard at informal gatherings called *rumbas* or *rumbones*. The rumba guaguanco has deep roots in Afro-Cuban music as well as influence in Latin American music, pop rock, Latin rock, and R & B music since the 1940s. A traditional percussion ensemble consists of three drummers, a clave player and someone playing the palitos (sticks) on a hard surface or cascara (the drum shell). The following Rumba Guaguanco has the traditional combination of instruments with additional drums. *Rumba Time* starts with four bars of improvisation, and on the fifth bar, the 3–2 rumba-style clave starts with three beats in its first bar. Notice that the third beat of the clave is on the "and" of 4. This is the only difference from the traditional 3–2 *son clave* that strikes on beat 4.

Rumba Time

Chalo Eduardo

Brazilian-Maracatu Baque Virado

Found in the northern Brazilian State of Pernambuco, this traditional folkloric Afro-Brazilian celebration of African nations is descended from the Christmas festivities on sugar plantations during the colonial period. Dressing in European court costumes as lords and ladies, these groups performed dance dramas featuring a procession of kings, queens and their court. During Carnaval, this kind of ensemble group parades in the city of Recife to a slow moving rhythm, dancing and singing to a hypnotic beat. Groups date back to the nineteenth century. Maracatu Leao Coroado and Maracatu Elefante are among the oldest groups in this tradition. The percussion ensemble plays an intricate counter rhythm known as the *baque virado* at a slow- to medium-tempo with surdos called *zabumbas*, snares called *tarols*, bells/gongue and agogos.

Maracatu Baque Virado

Chalo Eduardo

chapter ten:
world beat ensembles

This chapter builds percussion ensembles based on the key patterns and exercises found in previous chapters of this book. The arrangements are based on culturally specific rhythms. Much music of today in some way, shape or form incorporates rhythms from cultures around the world. This is where the term "world rhythm" or "world percussion" got its birth. Here, you can learn what professional percussionists do when creating original percussion ensembles using the rhythms of the world. Drum substituting happens all the time, so feel free to use what you have. Remember that all rhythms can be played on any instrument.

Building a World Percussion Ensemble

Here are three suggestions to help you build your world percussion ensemble.

1. Choose the lead instrument that will cue all cadences, call and responses, breaks, call-ins and call-outs.

2. Increase ensemble size by doubling similar instruments to create instrument sections.

3. Use dynamics! Listen to the entire ensemble and the relationship of each individual pattern within the overall sound.

Choosing Instruments and Rhythms

Create your own percussion piece using the rhythms and instruments found in previous chapters. Choose one instrument from each instrument family or chapter, and select a rhythm for that instrument to play. Following are some ideas for composing your own ensemble piece.

Formal Structure

Introduction, Call and Response

Call In—Section A

    All Play

Call Out—Section B

    Solos

    All Play

Call Out—End

Introduction, Call and Response

Introductions can be predetermined or improvised. The lead instrument directs *the Call and Response*, a technique during which the lead drummer plays a rhythm and the same rhythm is repeated by the entire ensemble in musical time.

Call In/Call Out

The *Call In* and *Call Out* are generally the same rhythm each time. This rhythm is predetermined and should be easily heard and recognized by the ensemble.

The leader plays the *Call In* to *Section A*, where the entire ensemble plays together (*All Play*).

Section B Solos—Individual or Section

Options for Section B solos:

1. Set the length of the solo, or play open-ended to be cued by the lead drummer with the *Call In* back to *Section A*.

2. Choose a unison break to be played by the entire ensemble during the solo. The lead drummer performs the *Call In* cue back to *Section A*.

3. The lead drummer plays through the ensemble rhythm, cueing *Call and Response*. The ensemble performs the responses, and the lead drummer plays the *Call In* cue back to *Section A*.

Performance Tips

Because there is so much going on at the same time, it is important to always listen to everyone and keep focused on the leader directing the ensemble using rhythmic cues. The leader must keep eye contact with the ensemble and the ensemble must keep eye contact with the leader. A whistle or hand movement can precede any call. Experiment by combining any of the options given for solos in *Section B*.

Solo Tips

The soloist plays but the leader calls in. During the solo, the leader can choose one or more unison lines to be played by the ensemble on every other bar. Solos can feature an entire section or individual players. Don't bash, and always use dynamics.

Call of the Drums

Here is an arrangement using rhythms introduced in this book with the addition of some new rhythmic patterns.

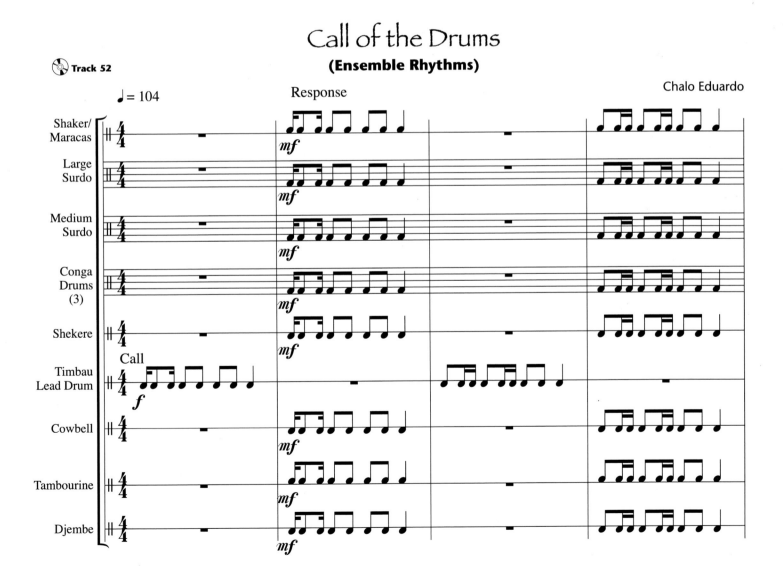

World Piece

Create drumming ensembles using rhythms you have composed as well as rhythms you have heard from around the globe. Experiment with instrument and rhythmic combinations.

World Piece

Frank Kumor

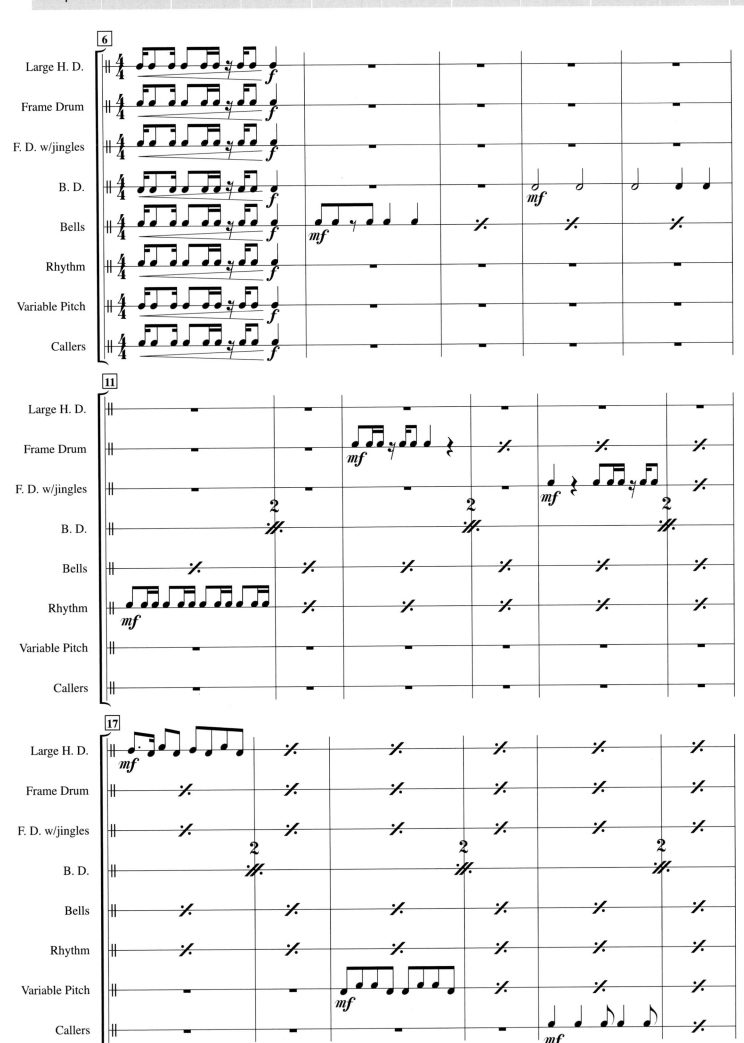

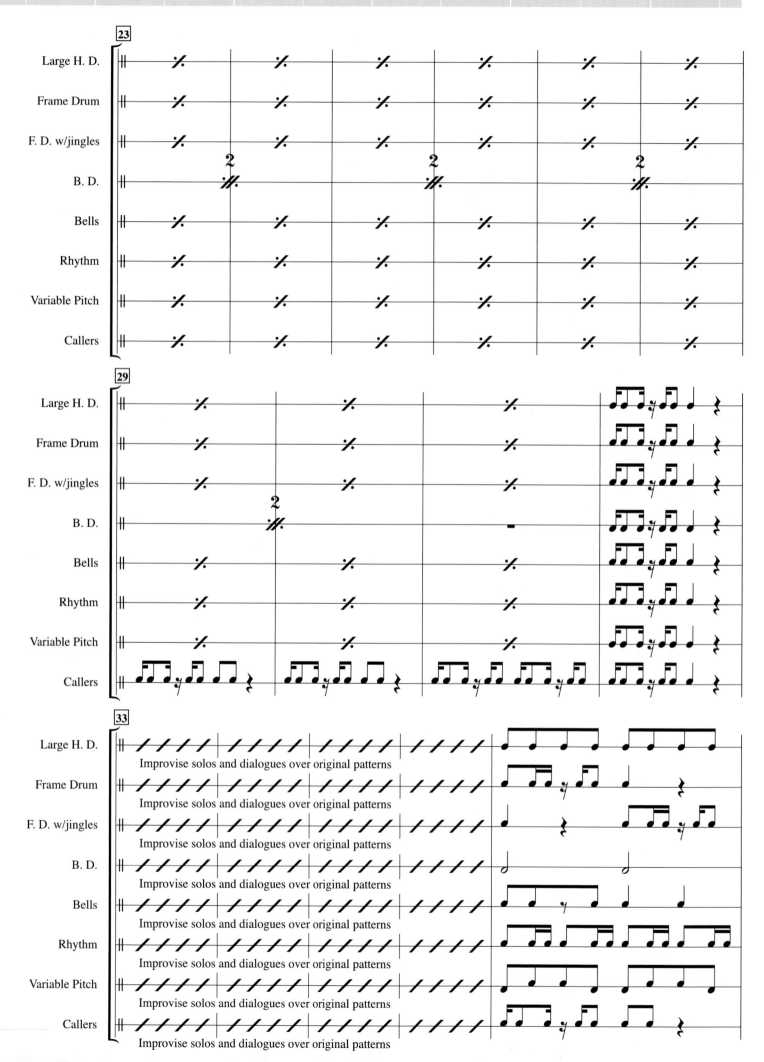

Enjoy your journey around the World of Percussion!

about the authors

Chalo Eduardo's experience as a bandleader, recording artist and entertainer, combined with his significant contributions to a variety of music styles, has led to associations with world-class musical artists such as Gloria Estefan, Mickey Hart, Bruce Hornsby, Gato Barbieri and many others. Chalo's ten-year association with Sergio Mendes as a featured performer gained him international acclaim for his showmanship, fiery solos, and center-stage tambourine juggling and dancing performances, leading to his participation in events such as San Francisco's huge New Year's Eve (SFNYE) event, Tribute to Santana's at L.A.'s Rockawalk and, in Atlanta, at a concert produced in association with the 1996 Olympics. His expertise is evidenced in his creation of a signature line of Brazilian percussion instruments manufactured by Remo.

Chalo has recorded two albums under his own leadership, *I Miss Rio* and *Samba Nova*, both on Carnaval Records. He has also contributed to numerous projects for artists including vocalists Kevin Letteu, Mark Murphy and Mickey Hart Suptralingue, as well as soundtracks for Sega video games and commercials for both radio and TV. Having played and organized drum ensembles for 15 years, he performed and choreographed drummers and dancers for the 1999 and 2000 Grammy Awards with Ricky Martin.

Chalo's reputation as a consummate percussionist and performer continues to precede him, bringing him to the attention of artists, producers, concert promoters, and recording companies wherever his exuberance, polished performance, percussive expertise, versatility, and efficiency are required.

Frank Kumor is currently on the music faculty at Kutztown University of Pennsylvania and is completing a Doctor of Musical Arts in Percussion Performance at the University of Kentucky in Lexington. Mr. Kumor served as a part-time faculty member and graduate teaching assistant at the University of Kentucky, teaching music theory and percussion and acting as assistant conductor of the university's percussion ensemble, African ensemble and steel band.

The ensembles lead by Mr. Kumor at Kutztown University perform music of West Africa, South Africa, Brazil and the Middle East, and are regularly invited to be featured performers for school programs and events in the Pennsylvania and New Jersey areas. In 1999, the Kutztown University World Percussion Ensemble was invited to perform at the FIFA Women's World Cup Fanfest Events at Giants Stadium in East Rutherford, New Jersey.

Mr. Kumor appears regularly at music conferences around the United States and serves on the keyboard committee for the Percussive Arts Society. He is a performing artist and clinician for Paiste Cymbals, Yamaha Percussion, Remo World Percussion, Gambal Mallets, Johnny Rabb Drumsticks and Alfred Publishing Company.